# GLOBALIZATION
## Debts, Arms and Reforms in South Asia

## By the Same Author

- Education and Socio-economic Development: Rural Urban Divide in India and South Asia
- Indigenous Resources for Rural Development: Agricultural Mechanisation and Rural Industrialisation
- नौकरशाही का प्रबन्धः आर्थिक सुधारों एवं ग्रामीण विकास के लिए पुनर्गठन
- पुलिस एवं अदालतों में नागरिक सहभागिताः सस्ते-एवं-शीघ्र न्याय के लिए एक प्रशासनिक ढाँचा

---

**About the Author**

Before taking up a contractual assignment as Resident Consultant for one year with the N.P.I.U. for implementing the World Bank project under the Ministry of HRD, Government of India, **Dr. Sures Chandra Jain** had worked as Chief General Manager for nearly 20 years at M.P. Laghu Udyog Nigam (an undertaking of the Government of Madhya Pradesh) in Bhopal when he voluntarily retired in 2002. Dr. Jain had also worked for many multinational corporations like I.B.M., Massey-Ferguson, Atomic Energy of Canada Limited, and G.T.E. when he was in Canada and USA from 1970 to 1983. He was a visiting Fellow at UNESCO, Paris, France.

Dr. Jain obtained the degrees of Doctor of Education (Ph.D.) from Columbia University, New York, U.S.A. and B.I.S. from the University of Waterloo in Canada, Besides several research papers, Dr. Jain has written five books, two in Hindi and three in English, all of them published by Concept Publishing Company, New Delhi. He is either an author or co-author of many government reports which are not meant for general publication.

# GLOBALIZATION
## Debts, Arms and Reforms in South Asia

Dr. Sures Chandra Jain

CONCEPT PUBLISHING COMPANY, NEW DELHI-110059

**Cataloging in Publication Data—DK**
*Courtesy:* D.K. Agencies (P) Ltd. <docinfo@dkagencies.com>

**Jain, Sures Chandra,** 1946-
Globalization : debts, arms and reforms in South Asia/ Sures Chandra Jain.
p. cm.
Includes bibliographical references.
Includes index.
ISBN 8180691543

1. Globalization. 2. South Asia—Economic policy. 3. Debts, External—South Asia. 4. South Asia—Armed Forces Appropriations and expenditures. I. Title.

338.954 21



ISBN : 81-8069-154-3

First Published 2005



*Published and Printed by*
Ashok Kumar Mittal
**Concept Publishing Company**
A/15-16, Commercial Block, Mohan Garden
New Delhi-110059 (INDIA)

*Phone* : 25351460, 25351794
*Fax* : 091-11-25357103
*Email* : publishing@conceptpub.com

# Preface

The State control of the economy through licence, permit, quota, etc. is being given up in a phased manner, which has been the hallmark of policy right from independence in 1947 till the end of century. Since 1991, economic reforms are being initiated in India.

These attempts to liberalize the economy of India and many other developing countries are substantially based on foreign "debt", "aid", and "technology". The object of this book is to critically analyze the pitfalls associated with this dependence on foreign debt, aid and technology, which leads of perpetuating poverty. This situation has worsened with the arrival of so called *Globalization*. Frans J. Schuurman of the Institute of Development Studies at the University of Nijmegen in the Netherlands said "*...That if there ever was anything like globalization then that is already over because we have now entered a period of increasing fragmentation and de-globalization.*"

The foreign debt of India has doubled just in two years, from Rs. 1,28,451 crore in 1989-90 to Rs. 2,46,038 crore in 1991-92. This doubling of the debt is not reflected in dollar amount, because the Indian currency was substantially devalued in 1991. The value of the US dollar has also become twice in less than three years, from approximately Rs. 18 in 1991 to almost Rs. 32 during 1993-94, and reaching nearly Rs. 50 in 2002. The new loans are now being negotiated to pay for the interest on the previous loans.

Now, with this situation in the beginning of 2000s, India has been caught into the debt-trap, the way Mexico, Brazil and many other developing countries have been since the early 1980s. With this debt-trap, the speed and direction of the Indian economy, like that of many other developing countries, is also being substantially dictated by the International Monetary Fund (IMF) and the World Bank combine, the money-lending agencies effectively controlled by the Western powers. After all, the motives of the Western powers during colonialism were to exploit the economic resources of the colonies, which, in the aftermath of colonialism after the Second World War, are being done through the remote control of the IMF and the World Bank combine, which takes back more money in the form of interest on debt, creating social conflicts in developing countries and then selling arms forcing them to cut down expenditure on Health and Education, the basic necessities of life. An editorial in the *Hindustan Times*, New Delhi, 25-7-2000, lamented that:

> It is no secret that the debt burden is crippling the HIPCs' (Highly Indebted Poor Countries) efforts to sustain growth or to gain independence from the international financial institutions. While they are having to spend 10 per cent of their income on health and education, about 60 per cent is going towards servicing of the debt. ... *heavily indebted poor countries (HIPCs)...are spending $ 60 million a day towards debt servicing.*

What does this dependence on foreign debt mean for the sovereignty of the nation? It is simple and brutal: Just perpetuating poverty. This Book is primarily designed as a general reference material for the layman who wishes to become familiar with the subject of foreign debt, arms, international developmental agencies as an instrument of maintaining poverty and finally, the globalization and so called economic reforms, as they it relates with the overall socio-economic development of the country.

This book was originally written in 1982 when I was in Canada, updated and thoroughly revised ten years later in 1992, and now updated and revised again the same ten years later in 2002. As a result, some part of this book may in the first instance appear to be a bit disjointed but, in fact, analyses and arguments made 20 years ago and 10 years ago are even much more relevant today. This is precisely because expenditure on arms and debt servicing adversely affecting investment in health and education continue to be perennial problems and pressing issues facing India and other developing country. These problems of expenditure on arms and debt servicing adversely affecting investment in health and education have only gonė from bad to worse in these last 20 years when the book was originally written.

My wife, Dr. Krishna and our two little children, Nidhi and Amogh, who so gracefully provided with me what otherwise would have been their time.

Bhopal, **Sures Chandra Jain**
September 18, 2002

# Contents

# List of Tables

# Introduction

*...But I do not know of any country in the world which might have become prosperous with the help and formulae of the International Monetary Fund (IMF).*

*—Kuldip Nayar[1], 1991*

*"...That if there ever was anything like globalization then that is already over because we have now entered a period of increasing fragmentation and de-globalization."*

*—Frans J. Schuurman[2], 2001*

*"Globalization and destabilization are coinciding phenomena; a causal relationship is probable."*

*—Kristoffel Lieten[3], 2001*

*The upshot is that debt has become a form of bondage, and the indebted economies have become indentured economies—a clear manifestation of neo-colonialism.*

*—Julius K. Nyerere[4], 1990*

A number of policy planners and intellectuals in India and other formerly colonized countries, almost always look towards their old masters' ways and means and often seek their "guidance" and do so with rather gracious submission.

The policy planners and intellectuals in India are so Westernized in their outlook that they virtually develop a contempt for their native indigenous values and cultural traditions, and follow everything that is Western no matter however ridiculous, absurd and irrelevant. It is these policy planners and intellectuals who must seek foreign "aid" and global "interdependence", regardless of their disastrous socio-economic consequences.

There are several chapters in this book. It is a historical fact that what is now called the "Third World" is yesterday's colonized world, the world that was ruthlessly plundered and its inhabitants mercilessly dehumanized. Dr. Martin Luther King Jr., the slain civil rights leader of the blacks in the United States, a Nobel Laureate for Peace, said[5]:

> "We in the West must bear in mind that the poor countries are poor primarily because we have exploited them through political or economic exploitation."

Those individuals in India and the Third World who seek foreign "aid" and global "interdependence" continue to ignore, basically for their selfish reasons, what is now a very well-documented fact that foreign aid has contributed nothing as far as the development of the nation is concerned. L.B. Pearson, former Prime Minister of Canada, a Nobel Laureate for Peace[6], said:

> "On the whole, the evidence suggests that economic assistance has, at best, made little contribution to the aided nations' growth and, at worst, has seriously distorted it... (Aid) too, perpetuates what is in essence a colonial relationship."

This gloomy picture shows that we have reached the ironic state "Who aids whom". The total outflows from India and the developing countries have already begun to exceed the amount of capital receipts coming from abroad. Table 1 shows External Debt, Military Expenditure percentage of GNP, Public Expenditure on Education and Health of the Various Regions of the World for 2000. Debt is ever increasing, reaching $ 100 billion in 2001 (Rs. 4,67,589 crores) and interest being paid is between Rs. 5000 to 6000 crore every year during the decade of so called reforms since 1991. The value of one $ in 1981 was Rs. 7.81, which increased to 17.94 in decade later in 1991, which further jumped to Rs. 48 in another decade in 2001. During the ten years of reforms from 1991 to 2001, the value of one $ became nearly three times. The highly indebted poor countries suffer the brunt of military spending[7]:

"It is no secret that the debt burden is crippling the HIPCs' (Highly Indebted Poor Countries) efforts to sustain growth or to gain independence from the international financial institutions. While they have to spend 10 per cent of their income on health and education, about 60 per cent is going towards servicing of the debt. ...*Heavily indebted poor countries (HIPCs)...are spending $ 60 million a day towards debt servicing.*"

Mortgage the nation's economic control with the Western money lenders! Why not? After all, the State in India is the "personal property", as Arun Shourie[8], a noted scholar and an eminent journalist, remarked. There is apparently no need to mention the national humiliation that goes with this kind of borrowing. The agony of this whole scenario is pretty bizarre: the prospective nation first must carry a 'begging bowl', and if endowed with "charity" it must allow its economy's control and plunder by the moneylenders. Yet more bizarre is the fact that this exploitation is blatantly carried out under the philanthropic banner of "helping the helpless".

South Asia is the most militarized zone moving against the world trend. In South Asia countries, percentage of population living below the poverty may have come down in the decade from nearly 45 per cent in 1987 to 40 per cent in 1998, but the fact remains that the absolute number of them has increased from 475 million to 522 million. So at the current rate of progress in implementing the poverty alleviation schemes, the poverty would never be out of the face of the South Asia. Most of the poor of the World live in South Asia as reported by the World Bank[9]:

> ...Poor people are active agents in their lives, but are often powerless to influence the social and economic factors that determine their well-being. ...The world has deep poverty amid plenty. Of the world's 6 billion people (in the year 2000) 2.8 billion—almost half—live on less than $2 a day, and 1.2 billion—a fifth—live on less than $1 a day, with 44 per cent living in South Asia.

India's military budget for 2002-03 in Rs. 65,000 crore. The military expenditure of the entire World is $ 780 billion in 1999 (Rs. 37,44,000 crore).

The specific details and the statistical analysis of the transactions, e.g. aid received and payments on interest, amortization, debt servicing, repatriated profits, etc., appear in the appropriate sections in the text.[10]

The various chapters in this book deal with the role of so called foreign "aid" in the task of nation building, wherein we have reached the ironic state of "who aids whom". If we simply put on one side of the scale the total inflow of money from the rich nations, the so called aid-givers, and on the other side the total outflow of money from the poor nations, the so called aid-seekers, it turns out that it is the poor nations who actually aid the rich nations by way of interest and amortization on borrowed money, money repatriated by multinational corporations, money paid to import the generally obsolete technology, and money paid to purchase arms, etc.

**Table I.1:** External Debt, Military Expenditure percentage of GNP, Public Expenditure on Education and Health of the Various Regions of the World for 2000

| *Region* | *External Debt $ Millions 1998* | *Military Expenditure % of GNP 1997* | *Public Expenditure on education % of GNP 1997* | *Public expenditure on health % of GDP 1990-98* |
|---|---|---|---|---|
| | *WDR P 315* | *WDR P 307* | *WDR P 285* | *WDR P 287* |
| World | -- | 2.5 | 4.8 | 2.5 |
| Low Income | 579,545 | 2.9 | 3.3 | 1.3 |
| Middle Income | 1,956,501 | 2.9 | 4.8 | 3.1 |
| Low and Middle Income | 2,536,046 | 2.9 | 4.1 | 1.9 |
| East Asia and Pacific | 667,522 | 2.5 | 2.9 | 1.7 |
| Europe and Central Asia | 480,539 | 4.0 | 5.1 | 4.0 |
| Latin America and Caribbean | 786,019 | 1.8 | 3.6 | 3.3 |
| Middle East and North Africa | 208,059 | 7.0 | 5.2 | 2.4 |
| South Asia | 163,775 | 3.1 | 3.1 | 0.8 |
| Sub-Saharan Africa | 230,132 | 2.3 | 4.1 | 1.5 |

*Source:* The World Bank, *World Development Report 2000/2001*, Oxford University Press, New York, 2000.

The multinational corporations, which are now being increasingly promoted to start their operations in India and other Third World countries, no doubt barely cater to the consumer needs of the 2 to 5 per cent of the upper crust of the population in return for which these multinational corporations repatriate profits, utilize our market as a waste bin, a dumping ground for their largely discarded and/or environmentally dangerous technology. Now, with the so called opening of the economy to the world in general and to India in particular since the middle of 1991 by increasing de-regulation of industries, these multinational corporations would obviously have no regard for the fact that India's industrial infrastructure is to be based on self-reliance and the development of indigenous technology, if India is to develop in the long run. For example, by inviting multinational corporations to open their industries in India for manufacturing soft drinks, potato chips, chicken, etc., are we not depriving our native industrial entrepreneurs with an opportunity of developing their products? How can a struggling Indian entrepreneur, who is manufacturing soft drinks, can compete with the multinational giants manufacturing Pepsi and Coca Cola?

There are five chapters in this book.

Chapter 1 deals with the colonial legacy. This chapter deals with how, in the aftermath of the disintegration of the colonial rule after the Second World War in 1945, the various western powers through the media of so called international developmental agencies have taken the control of the economy of their former colonies. In the 1960s, these international developmental agencies worked under the aegis of first UN Development Decade, which did not produce any tangible developmental gains in the interest of the poor countries.

Probably having this fact in mind and also the lessons from the failures of the first UN Development Decade, in 1970, the UN International Development Strategy for the 1970s was launched. This strategy was based upon the then published

(1969) Pearson Report on the theme of International Development based on and the UNCTAD-I and UNCTAD-II resolutions. Unfortunately enough, neither the recommendations made in the Pearson Report nor the UNCTAD resolutions have been carried out. This strategy was dead even before its scheduled mid-term review in 1975. For the 1980s, we have the Brandt Commission Report, and for the 1990s we have the South Commission Report (details on these various Reports are given later and also in the text in Chapter 4). In terms of economic relations between developed and developing countries, the developing countries have been left with the following three alternatives:

1. Let the present international monetary system and the monopoly of the developed market economies continue,
2. Cut themselves off from the above alternative and make 'profits' from 'losses' of 'aid' and 'investment' as discussed earlier, or
3. To make a clean break from the alternative No.1, and follow a rough course of 'go it alone, involving the highest degree of bitterness and frustration, the way the Chinese accomplished in the aftermath of Communist take-over, and practiced in Tanzania but without success.

Chapter 2 deals with the quantitative figures of the foreign debt and aid from the 1950s to 1990s. The mounting amount of debts and subsequent negotiations of new loans to pay for the interests of the previous loans is a precarious situation.

Debt of India is ever-increasing from 1980 onwards, and skyrocketing since 1991 when the so called reforms began. This debt reached $ 100 billion in 2001 (Rs. 4,67,589 crores) and interest being paid is between Rs. 5000 to 6000 crore every year during the decade of so called reforms since 1991. The value of one $ in 1981 was Rs. 7.81, which increased to 17.94 in a decade later in 1991, which further jumped to Rs. 48 in another decade in 2001. During the ten years of reforms from 1991 to 2001, the value of one $ became nearly three times. The highly indebted poor countries suffer the brunt of military spending[11] :

> "It is no secret that the debt burden is crippling the HIPCs' (Highly Indebted Poor Countries) efforts to sustain growth or to gain independence from the international financial institutions. While they have to spend 10 per cent of their income on health and education, about 60 per cent is going towards servicing of the debt. ...*Heavily indebted poor Countries (HIPCs)...are spending $ 60 million a day towards debt servicing.*"

Mortgage the nation's economic control with the Western moneylenders! Why not? After all, the State in India is the "personal property", as Arun Shourie[12], a noted scholar and an eminent journalist, remarked. This statement of Shourie is much more true now 20 years later now than when it was said in 1980 when India had negotiated a big loan at that time from the World Bank and the IMF. There is apparently no need to mention the national humiliation that goes with this kind of borrowing. The agony of this whole scenario is pretty bizarre: the prospective nation first must carry a 'begging bowl', and if endowed with "charity" it must allow its economy's control and plunder by the moneylenders. Yet more bizarre is the fact that this exploitation is blatantly carried out under the philanthropic banner of "helping the helpless".

The above figures are discussed and put in Tables in the text of Chapter 2(B) of this book, all taken from various Government of India documents and the World Bank.

These increases in the amount of debt, amount of interest, debt service ratio and foreign exchange rate without any doubt indicate that India in the early 1990s has been caught in debt-trap, as have been Mexico, Brazil and many other developing countries since the 1980s. After getting India into debt-trap in the early 1990s, the World Bank and the IMF combine is also controlling the speed and direction of the Indian economy.

What used to be done by the Western powers during the colonial period of Asian, African and Latin American poor countries, is now being done through the IMF and the World Bank combine, the money-lender agencies effectively controlled by the Western powers.

After all, the motives of the Western Powers during colonialism were to exploit the economic resources of the colonies. Now, in the aftermath of the colonialism after the Second World War, this economic exploitation of the former colonies is being done through the remote control of the IMF and the World Bank combine.

What does this dependence on foreign debt mean for the sovereignty of the nation?

With this much money being paid back to the developed nations through the World Bank and IMF combine, the poor countries are simply not left with bare necessary resources for the funding of their various socio-economic developmental projects. This huge interest on debts is a drain on the country's resources, not to mention the money repatriated by the multinational corporations of the Western countries.

A New York-based think-tank, North South Round Table (NSRT), in its findings, categorically stated in 1993 that the IMF and the World Bank have failed to provide social and economic security for most of the world's people.

Kuldip Nayar, a noted journalist of India, rightly stated in *Rajasthan Patrika*, Jaipur, on 17-7-1991[13]:

> "...But I do not know of any country in the world, which might have become prosperous with the help and formulae of the International Monetary Fund (IMF)." (Translated from the Hindi by the author)

In view of the above, the problem is how the developing countries can achieve economic independence after having been politically independent from the colonial rulers. J.K. Nyerere[14], a widely acknowledged authority on the problems of the Third World countries, wrote:

> "To burden the people with the big loans, the repayment of which will be beyond their means, is not to help them but to make them suffer..."

The rich countries, through a mechanism of highly complicated jargon of phraseology by which they calculate the figures of debt, aid, amortization, principals and interests, etc. of the developing countries, and the developed countries through the International Monetary Fund and the World Bank combine have begun to control the economies of not only the smaller countries in the developing world but also the giants among them such as Brazil, Mexico, Argentina in the 1980s and have now also got in their paws India as well since the beginning of 1990s. What was the pathetic situation of the Latin American giants in the 1980s, has begun to happen in India in 1990s, for heavy borrowings by India from the IMF and the World Bank since 1985 in general, and from 1991 in particular, are clearly based on the fact that India had to give the control and direction of the Indian economy in the hands of the IMF and the World Bank combine. There has been several instances, where the Finance Minister of India since middle of 1991 had been writing to the IMF and the World Bank, giving them full assurance in writing in advance of the policies to be adopted by the Government of India. One such letter was written on November 11, 1991. The text of the letter is produced in Chapter 2(C) of this book. Lal Krishna Advani[15], an eminent political leader of India and President of Bharatiya Janata Party made the following observations while commenting on the liberalization policy of the Government, which began since the middle of 1991:

> "Our party is committed to liberalization, but there is a Government that talks of liberalization in a manner so as to make our entire economic approach subject to the dictates of the IMF and the World Bank."

Chapter 3 deals with the expenditure incurred by India and other developing countries on armaments and arms imports *vis-à-vis* health and education, etc. The total amount of expenditure on arms is over $ 1000 billion every year. This is a fact of life that only a small amount of current expenditure on arms is sufficient for the eradication of literacy and for providing basic health care needs and malnutrition of the entire developing world. The expenditure on arms manufacturing and for importing of arms is one of the major sources of the debts of the poor countries.

For example, the money spent by India on defence is nearly 4 times that of the combined expenditure on health, education, and rural development[16], when the improvement of our socio-economic conditions is most essential for equity and social justice.

Yet, at the same time, given the perception of threats at India's border right from China's invasion in 1962, Pakistan's attack in 1965, and India's involvement in the erstwhile east wing of Pakistan (now Bangladesh) on the one hand, and the growing unrest within the country since early 1980s, on the other, it is obviously not possible to cut down expenditure on defence without risking the security of the country itself.

India's military budget for 2002-03 was Rs. 65,000 crore. The military expenditure of the entire world was $ 780 billion in 1999[17] (Rs. 37,44,000 crore).

> "Total world military expenditure rose 2.1 per cent in real terms in 1999 after a long period of decline... The United States, Russia, China and France accounted for most of the global increase but countries spending relatively the most on guns are the emerging economies... *Arms spending totalled about $780 billion in 1999.* ...The countries with the heaviest economic burden on military expenditure are generally poor countries involved in armed conflict and/ or located in areas of tension."

The political changes in the world have been far too sweeping since 1989. Communism is dead in the countries of Eastern Europe. The erstwhile USSR has been converted into a Commonwealth of Independent States (CIS). Communism is now in the books of history. East and West Germany have been united into a single State. Efforts are made to economically unite the countries in Europe with a single currency, etc. This rapidly changing political environment of the World has certainly been in the positive direction for international peace, but it is not necessary for international security. Nevertheless, with this positive international environment, if the leaders of the world community, particularly USA and countries in Europe, heed the recommendations of the Brandt (1980) and South Commission (1990) Reports, the world would be a better place to live in both for the developed and the developing countries. The plight of the HIPCs' (Highly Indebted Poor Countries) regarding the amount of interest on debts and expenditure on health and education is quite disturbing[18] (For details on these Reports, see Chapter 4):

> It is no secret that the debt burden is crippling the HIPCs' (Highly Indebted Poor Countries) efforts to sustain growth or to gain independence from the international financial institutions. While they have to spend 10 per cent of their income on health and education, about 60 per cent is going towards servicing of the debt. ...*Heavily indebted poor Countries (HIPCs)...are spending $ 60 million a day towards debt servicing.*

Chapter 4 deals with the role of international developmental agencies in transforming the economic lot of the developing economies.

We notice that the following International Reports have been published from 1950s to 1990s on the development of issues in the Third World:

1. For the 1950s: The United Nations Development Decade I. It failed miserably.
2. For the 1960s: The United Nations Development Decade-II. It too failed. It did not achieve its stated objectives.
3. For the 1970s: "Partners in Development", report of the Commission on International Development, commissioned by the World Bank, under the Chairmanship of L.B. Pearson, former Prime Minister of Canada, a Nobel Laureate for Peace. Recommendations of this report were dead even before their scheduled review.
4. For the 1980s: "North-South: A Programme for Survival" the report of the Independent Commission on

International Development Issues, under the Chairmanship of Willy Brandt, former Chancellor of the then West Germany and Nobel Prize winner for Peace.

In the Brandt Commission Report, an emergency programme for the upliftment of the developing countries for 1980-85 was spelled out, none of which has ever been implemented, such as[19],

"There must be substantial increase in the transfer of resources to developing countries in order to finance:

(a) Projects and programmes to alleviate poverty and to expand food production, especially in the least developed countries.

(b) Exploration and development of energy and mineral resources.

(c) Stabilization of the prices and earnings of commodity exports and expanded domestic processing of commodities."

5. For the 1990s: "The Challenge to the South", the Report of the South Commission, under the chairmanship of Julius K. Neyrere, former President of Tanzania and internationally acclaimed authority on developmental issues in the Third World. The Non-Aligned Movement sanctioned this Report in 1986 in Zimbabwe. (Dr. Man Mohan Singh, Finance Minister of India since 1991, was one of the principal authors of this Report).

In this Report[20], emphasis has been laid on cooperation within the developing world (i.e. the South, as mentioned in this Report) and a request has been made to the developed countries (i.e. the North as mentioned in this Report) to reduce the debt burden:

"The time has come therefore for effective multilateral action to scale down the debt and reduce the burden of debt service to tolerable levels. In most cases, the debt crisis has turned out to be a crisis of solvency rather than merely of liquidity. ...

> The upshot is that debt has become a form of bondage, and the indebted economies have become indentured economies—a clear manifestation of neo-colonialism. This state of affairs cannot go on. The debt and its service must be reduced to a level that allows growth to proceed at an acceptable pace. ...
>
> We reaffirm the need for an International Debt Conference with the participation of the debtor governments, the governments of the creditors, and the international financial institutions, whose mandate would be to arrive at a binding international agreement on a framework solution."

6. For the 2000s, the Millennium's first decade, United Nations Millennium Declaration.

The leaders of the World Community met at the United Nations and resolved to eradicate poverty from the face of Earth by 2015[21]:

### *The Millennium Declaration's Goals for Development and Poverty Eradication*

As the world entered the new millennium, heads of state and government gathered at the United Nations General Assembly to lay out their vision for the world. The leaders of the summit adopted the United Nations Millennium Declaration, recognizing their "collective responsibility to uphold the principles of human dignity, equality and equity at the global level". Among the many objectives set out by the declaration are specific, quantified and monitorable goals for development and poverty eradication by 2015:

- To halve the proportion of the world's people living on less than $1 a day.
- To halve the proportion of the world's people suffering from hunger.
- To halve the proportion of the world's people without access to safe drinking water.

- To achieve universal completion of primary schooling.
- To achieve gender equality in access to education.
- To reduce maternal mortality ratio by three quarters.
- To reduce under-five mortality rate by two-thirds.
- To halt and begin to reverse the spread of HIV/AIDS, malaria and other major diseases.

These goals build on the international development goals, which include three more targets—namely, to reduce infant mortality rate by two-thirds, to provide access for all who want reproductive health service and to implement national strategies for sustainable development by 2005 to reverse the loss of environment resources by 2015.

What are the prospects for achieving these goals?

As far as the implementation of the recommendations of these highly acclaimed international reports is concerned, nothing significant has been achieved right from the 1950s to the present year in the 1990s. The international developmental agencies, including that of the UN agencies such as the UNDP and the UNCTAD, have not even been able to scratch the surface. They have indeed often hampered the indigenous efforts of the developing countries, which remain under the illusion of assistance from these agencies.

As far as the role of the international developmental agencies in helping the socio-economic lot of the poor countries is concerned, it is the prior decision-making by the developed countries that carries in it the mechanics of guaranteed failure of the interests of the developing countries. This is the reason behind the failures of the international conferences and developmental agencies. The outcome of the whole conference usually turns out to be an illusion. Why an international illusion? Because the output results in three things at the end of the conferences:

1. The impractical resolutions, which in many cases are accepted by the underdeveloped nations reluctantly because they have no other choice;
2. The agreement to disagree and to arrange another conference (maybe up to four years), the UNCTAD, for

example. This, too, drags the issues out and sweeps the urgent and bare necessities of more than two-thirds of the people on earth under the political rug;

3. The collection of fresh statistics of the nations; how much poorer the nations have become, and how much more the rich nations have accumulated, thus ensuring that the economic gap goes on increasing.

Thus the realities of the whole exercise of the conference turn out to be like going to a circus or watching a theatre.

The three main policy generating 'isms' are liberalism, conservatism, and the so called radicalism. The development strategy of the poor nation has to be worked out in close coordination of all these three 'isms', for being liberal alone poses problems in implementation of the policies; being conservative alone and following the traditional way can no longer be accepted if we have to keep up pace with the technological renovations of today; and being radical may well create more problems than it could resolve. But we need radical policy recommendations to bring about the change, to break the stagnation, and to make the social systems dynamic and the move. The policy-generating machinery, so formulated, will produce the forces that will inevitably accelerate the development system.

Now let us look at some other alternatives to make the development assistance more effective. It should be designed in such a way as to be beneficial to both the donor and the recipient. One of the main reasons for the amount of money that is being repatriated to the donor nations is that this money simply could not be reinvested in these poor nations because of lack of business. Now the developed nations can do one thing to help establish small-scale industries that do not need much sophisticated technology, and the poor nations can then reinvest this repatriated money. After this, the developed nations should trade and import some manufactured goods from these poor countries. This would be beneficial to both groups, the developed and the underdeveloped, in a number of ways:

1. This reinvestment of what is repatriated today would help the developing nations in their struggle for economic independence. It would help move the take-off process towards self-sustained growth faster. It would help them in industrialization and urbanization, without much suffering from the scarcity of foreign exchange.
2. The scarcity of foreign exchange is more or less being financed by the developed nations in the form of loans and grants. With this reinvestment, these aids and grants would soon no longer be needed.
3. This would reduce the foreign borrowings, which cause the greatest danger that new loans could dry up and foreign exchange earnings fall.
4. This economic development of the underdeveloped, in this way, will serve the long-term interests of the developed nations. It will generate trade.
5. At the same time, the developing nations themselves will have to provide the political stability to encourage investment and to keep the tax rate at a lower level.

Aids, loans and grants, at this time proving to be not effective at all, could in the way mentioned above be a great contribution to both the developed and the underdeveloped. There would then emerge real peace and prosperity among all nations, without a burden being placed on any rich nation to provide 'aid'. Gunnar Myrdal says truly that trade, and not aid, will be the real test of intentions. Along with this, improved trade helps enrich social, political, and cultural environment as well.

Economic reforms as being initiated now since 1991 have not been able to bear fruits in more than a decade of their implementation[22]:

> "It has been argued that India had a restrictive, inward-looking regime, and that, therefore, the economic breakthrough could not come about. Beginning around 1980 with the first IMF, and speeded up with the radical

> changes in economic policy around 1990, India opted for an export-led and foreign-capital-driven development. The fruits of such development should have become visible, but they have not. The Indian upper middle classes have gained access to cable television, cellular phones, computers and king-size cigarettes. The goods remain by and large restricted to a one-digit percentage of the population. The vast majority of the population has hardly seen progress. GNP growth patterns have remained at the levels of the 1960s and 1970s, occasionally going up, as they did over the last two decades, attracting eulogies for the policy of liberalization, and then falling again, as they had done in the past."

Chapter 5 of this book is a conclusion, which illustrates the myth of the so called global interdependence. In this chapter, various policy alternatives have been examined, in which the role of aid and loan can become a catalyst for the development projects, if conditions are favourable to the underdeveloped nations.

In the various chapters in this book, the picture so far and the future prospects indicate conflict, non-coöperation, a gloomy outlook, and the frustrating desires on the part of the underdeveloped nations, precisely because we have not been fair enough to analyze all the problems facing the poor countries beyond our selfish interests. In spite of this gloomy picture, let us dare to be optimistic! I cannot see any reason why we cannot transform all these gloomy and frustrating outcomes into a positive contribution to help fight hunger and illiteracy, and provide shelter and clothing (the bare necessities and requirements of more than two-thirds of the people on earth over the three continents of Africa, Asia and Latin America). The fulfilling of these basic necessities and requirements will help create a feeling of human dignity and responsibility among these masses. This will eventually enable them to help themselves, in other words, to be self-reliant. The lawlessness, social disorders and unequal opportunity etc. are the phenomena that set the stages for change—change in existing socio-cultural value system. With the necessity of social change, an idea of revolution is inevitable. Revolution and brutality, especially the suppression of human freedom, are almost synonymous. But a planned revolution does not necessarily have to be brutal and barbaric to bring about social change and to create the required momentum necessary for it. This change, in terms of international development, can be made only through goodwill and unconditional international cooperation based upon mutual respect and peaceful coexistence among the nations involved within the existing UN system. In other words, it will mean that we have to adjust our national goals within the broad international economic system, as is being done in many developing countries after the disintegration of Communism in the erstwhile USSR and Europe in the late 1980s and the early 1990s.

In this regard, however, India and other developing countries must protect their national interests by adopting the following policy alternatives:

1. Since the middle of 1991, India is witnessing the liberalization of the economy, and subsequent reforms in the industrial sector. To harness the benefits of these reforms, it is equally important to have parallel reforms in the bureaucratic structure as well, which in essence still remains an extension of the British colonial administration, which had nothing to do with socio-economic development of the country. (This issue is beyond the scope of this book, about which I am writing separately.)
2. Economic reforms since 1991 should go on, but it should be kept in mind that it is nothing but a mirage to imagine that the country would develop on foreign debt, because the total outflow from the country has already begun to exceed the total inflow into the country, and that new loans are essentially being negotiated to pay the interest on the earlier loans.

In November 1997 the Institute of Development Studies of the University of Nijmegen in the Netherlands organized a workshop on the significance of globalization (as a concept, a theory, a discourse and/or as an ontological process) for development studies in developing countries. The following summary of the views of the many scholars who presented their papers in this workshop[23] :

Reinhart Kossler[24]: *"Globalization may be considered a complex and multi-dimensional set of processes of rapid change, while at the same time delineating a programme of fundamental and multi-dimensional change and an ideology to legitimize such change."*

Frans J. Schúurman[25]: *"...That if there ever was anything like globalization then that is already over because we have now entered a period of increasing fragmentation and de-globalization."*

Kristoffel Lieten[26]: *"Globalization and destabilization are coinciding phenomena; a causal relationship is probable."*

Reinhart Kossler[27]: *"In a time of enhanced globalization, inequality of life chances and life levels on a world scale has become an ever more acute problem."*

Ton van Naerssen[28]: *"Global cities are not only sites for the accumulation of capital but also major sites for the creation of a new global culture. It is in these cities, and particularly in the world cities, that new cultural and political identities are being constructed."*

Frans J. Schuurman[29]: *"...Globalization is...primarily cultural in nature. ...Traditional identities are under threat, indigenous people are alienated from their cultural heritage through the global movement of consumer capitalism."*

Kristoffel Lieten[30]: *"Beginning around 1980 with the first IMF, and speeded up with the radical changes in economic policy around 1990, India opted for an export-led and foreign-capital-driven development. The fruits of such development should have become visible, but they have not."*

So this process of economic liberalization should not be made synonymous with dependence on the IMF and the World Bank, or, as discussed earlier in this Preface and also in the text in Chapter 2(C) of this book, this would turn India from the present position of debt-trap into a Banana Republic.

If the above policy alternatives were honestly translated into action, it would then certainly remove poverty, what we have not been able to remove in India for nearly the last five decades since Independence in 1947.

The data analyzed in this book are mainly from India, South Asian countries, China, and the developing countries as a whole. The analysis in the book is applicable to India and South Asian countries in particular, and to the Third World in general.

The nations in the South Asian region, particularly India, Bangladesh, Pakistan and Sri Lanka, share the same colonial heritage. All these nations are the classical victims of:

1. The divide-and-rule policy of the British colonial domination, and
2. The socio-economic neo-colonialism being practiced by the western countries after direct political colonialism in the aftermath of Second World War.

Since we have now been free from colonialism for over four decades, there is a little point in putting the blame on these former colonizers, for it is we ourselves who form our own polity and developmental policies with an urban bias, largely based on western style. Hence, an all-out effort to strengthen civil society in South Asia under the chairmanship of the former prime minister of India I.K. Gujaral[31] is a commendable step in the right direction:

> We have before us the experience of detente between the East and the West and the confidence-building measures undertaken by two sides of divided Europe through the Helsinki process that finally led to the end of the Cold War, the establishment of the Organization for Security and Cooperation in Europe (OSCE). The Europeans were able to overcome the animosities created through two world wars and centuries of intra-European wars.
>
> Eminent personalities from India, Bangladesh, Bhutan, Maldives, Nepal, Pakistan and Sri Lanka have formed a citizens' commission for South Asia and brought out a joint declaration after their first meeting in Kathmandu on December 1-3, 2000. The chairperson of the group is former Prime Minister Inder Kumar Gujral and includes personalities with both stature and credibility not only in their respective countries but also in the world outside. The objective of the commission is a very laudable one, to stress the major role and responsibility of civil society in creating a favourable opinion for promotion of regional cooperation. It has urged the governments, opinion-makers and civil society of the SAARC member countries to reaffirm their political will to work collectively for peace, progress and prosperity with a view to improving the quality of life of one-fifth of humankind.

## NOTES

1. Kuldip Nayar, *Rajasthan Patrika* (Hindi Daily), Jaipur, 17-7-1991; p. 6. This passage of Nayar has been translated by the author from the original in Hindi. Nayar is an eminent journalist of India.
2. Frans J. Schuurman, Globalization and Development Studies: Introducing the Challenges, in Frans J. Schuurman, Ed., *Globalization and Development Studies: Challenges for the 21st Century*, Vistaar Publications (A division of Sage Pub.), New Delhi, 2001, p. 8.

3. Kristoffel Lieten, Multinationals and Development: Revisiting the Debate, in Frans J. Schuurman, Ed., *Globalization and Development Studies: Challenges for the 21st Century*, Vistaar Publications (A division of Sage Pub.), New Delhi, 2001, p. 104.
4. *The Challenge to the South: The Report of the South Commission*, (New York: Oxford University Press, 1990); p. 227.

   This Report of the South Commission, sanctioned by the Non-Aligned Movement (NAM) in 1986 in Zimbabwe, was prepared under the chairmanship of the former President of Tanzania, Julius K. Nyerere.

   India's Dr. Man Mohan Singh, former Governor of the Reserve Bank of India, and Minister of Finance since 1991, was one of the principal authors of this Report.
5. Dr. Martin Luther King, Jr., *Conscience for Change*, Canadian Broadcasting Corporation, Toronto, 1967; p. 36.
6. Lester Bowles Pearson, *Pearson on Pearson Report*, CERES, FAO Review on Development, Rome, Italy, March-April 1970; pp. 20, 24. The "Pearson Report" is a document prepared under the Chairmanship of L.B. Pearson, former Prime Minister of Canada, a Nobel Laureate for Peace, to outline the strategies for the development of the Third World's poverty-stricken people. This Report was commissioned by the World Bank. The report is titled "Partners in Development", (New York: Praeger Pub., 1969).
7. Editorial, Blessed are the poor, *Hindustan Times*, New Delhi, 25-7-2000, p. 15.
8. Arun Shourie, "The State As Personal Property", *The Economic and Political Weekly*, Bombay, March 8, 1980; p. 509.
9. The World Bank, *World Development Report 2000/2001*, Oxford University Press, New York, 2000, p. 3. The poverty line is $1.08 a day at 1993 PPP.
10. For details and tables on data and their sources, see *Chapter 2(B)* and *Chapter* 3 of this book.
11. Editorial, Blessed are the poor, *Hindustan Times*, New Delhi, 25-7-2000, p. 15.
12. Arun Shourie, "The State As Personal Property", *The Economic and Political Weekly*, Bombay, March 8, 1980; p. 509.
13. Kundip Nayar, *Rajasthan Patrika* (Hindi Daily), Jaipur, 17-7-1991; p. 6. This passage of Nayar has been translated by the author from the original in Hindi. Nayar is an eminent journalist of India.
14. This statement was made in the Arusha Declaration. Julius K. Nyerere, *Freedom and Socialism*, (Dar-es-Salaam: Oxford University Press, 1968); p. 240.

15. *Economic Times*, New Delhi, 10-8-1993, p. 2. In this article in the *Economic Times*, L.K. Advani has expressed his views on a wide range of issues dealing with the liberalization of Indian economy.
16. For details regarding various data on investments in health, education and armaments, see Chapter 3 of this book.
17. SIPRI, World's arms expenditure rising, *Times of India*, New Delhi, 15-6-2000, p. 16.
18. Editorial, *Blessed are the poor*, *Hindustan Times*, New Delhi, 25-7-2000, p. 15.
19. *North-South: A Programme for Survival*, Cambridge: The MIT Press, 1980; p. 290.
20. *The Challenge to the South*: The Report of the South Commission, New York: Oxford University Press, 1990, pp. 226-28.

    This Report, sanctioned by Non-Aligned Movement (NAM) in 1986 in Zimbabwe,was prepared by the South Commission under the chairmanship of the former president of Tanzania, Julius K. Nyerere. India's Dr. Man Mohan Singh, former Governor of the Reserve Bank of India, and Minister of Finance since 1991, was one of the principal authors of this Report. Dr. Man Mohan Singh, in his capacity as Finance Minister of India since June 1991, is without doubt the single force, backed-up by Prime Minister P.V. Narasimha Rao, of course, who has caused the foreign debt of India to become twice just in two years, from Rs. 1,28,451 crore in 1989-90 to Rs. 2,66,167 crore in 1991-92. This debt has doubled partly by borrowing heavily and partly by devaluing the Indian currency in 1991, at the behest of the IMF and the World Bank combine.
21. *Human Development Report 2001*, UNDP, Oxford University Press, New York, 2001, pp. 21, 24.
22. Kristoffel Lieten, Multinationals and Development: Revisiting the Debate, in Frans J. Schuurman, Ed., *Globalization and Development Studies: Challenges for the 21st Century*, Vistaar Publications (A division of Sage Pub.), New Delhi, 2001, p. 112.
23. The proceedings were published in Frans J. Schuurman, Ed., *Globalization and Development Studies: Challenges for the 21st Century*, Vistaar Publications (A division of Sage Pub.), New Delhi, 2001.
24. Reinhart Kossler, *Globalization and Human Rights: Some Developmental Reflections*, in *Ibid.*, p. 83.
25. Frans J. Schuurman, *Globalization and Development Studies: Introducing the Challenges*, in *Ibid.*, p. 8.
26. Kristoffel Lieten, *Multinationals and Development: Revisiting the Debate*, in *Ibid.*, p. 104.
27. Reinhart Kossler, *Globalization and Human Rights: Some Developmental Reflections*, in *Ibid.*, p. 90.

28. Ton van Naerssen, *Cities and the Globalization of Urban Development Policy*, in *Ibid.*, p. 183.
29. Frans J. Schuurman, *The Nation-State, Emancipatory Spaces and Development Studies in the Global Era*, p. 63.
30. Kristoffel Lieten, *Multinationals and Development: Revisiting the Debate*, p. 112.
31. K. Subrahmanyam, A Citizens' Commission: Strengthen Civil Society in South Asia, *Times of India*, New Delhi, 18-12-2000, p. 12.

# 1

# Introduction: The Colonial Legacy

*We in the West must bear in mind that the poor countries are poor primarily because we have exploited them through political or economic colonialism.*

*—Dr. Martin Luther King[1], Jr., 1967*

The object in this book is to analyze why the developing countries, the so called the "Third World", are poverty-stricken. It is historical fact that these nations, the "jewel" of which was India, as the imperialist Sir Winston Churchill said, have been blatantly exploited, both economically and politically. The Rev. Dr. Martin Luther King[2], Jr., said in 1967:

> We in the West must bear in mind that the poor countries are primarily poor because we have exploited them through political or economic colonialism.

Towards this end, the "contribution" of foreign debt, aid and arms is to be analyzed in the task of nation-building in India, South Asian countries in particular, and in the developing countries in general, formerly under the colonial control of the Western countries.

After the disintegration of colonialism in the aftermath of Second World War, the rich nations undertook to help their former colonial countries to develop economically. Now the question arises as to why these rich countries should seek to help other nations when even the richest of them is saddled with fairly acute social and economic problems within its own borders? The answer is: "The fullest possible utilization of all the world's resources, human and physical, which can be brought about only by international cooperation, helps not only these countries now economically weak but also those strong and wealthy", as L.B. Pearson[3], the former Prime Minister of Canada, stated. Now the question arises: how this so called "Third World" emerged and why these nations of Africa, Asia and Latin America are poverty-stricken? I would cite two transitional processes:

1. From former colonies and slavery to political freedom and the national liberation, and
2. From this national liberation to a struggle towards economic liberation.

These two transitional processes have to be analyzed in a rather unique perspective. The former process involved the problem of how to achieve the self-image, identity, human dignity and political liberation from their former rulers. The latter process, which is going on now, poses the problems of how to keep up and maintain this self-identity, human dignity and political independence achieved after struggling so hard with so much sacrifice for centuries, and how to be one's own master in a real and practical way, without being influenced by external pressures in discharging domestic affairs and international responsibilities. At the same time, this must be done without putting extra and undue economic pressures upon the rich nations in the form of aids and grants. These two processes are transitional processes, but they are naturally linked with the Western capitalistic welfare states, since these poor nations, forming the so called "Third World", were the colonies of the West. However, the latter transitional process from national liberation to economic independence is based upon mutual social, cultural and economic interests. Business-like deals, now and then, lead to bitter confrontation between the two groups—One group is called underdeveloped, the former colonies; the other is called developed, the former rulers.

The two rivals, the United States and the former USSR, were involved the cold war in 1950s and 1960s, with both having equal destructive power at their disposal and both practicing entirely different socio-cultural value-systems in their political administrative structures.

The two rivals began to realize that each possessed enough military arsenal to annihilate the other and to blow this earth itself up many times over. They thought that neither of them was likely to 'celebrate' the victory. All that each would watch would be the disintegration of human bodies at an unprecedented scale, burned by nuclear radiation. Maurice Strong, a noted Canadian citizen pointed out that "civilizations have been menaced before, but this is the first time that the entire world has been threatened."

Having realized the capacity of annihilating each other and living under a constant fear and horror of war, the two rivals began to come closer to cooperation during the 1970s and 1980s. In the late 1980s, particularly in 1989, 1990 and 1991, communism came to an abrupt end in Eastern Europe and in the former USSR. The latter, in December 1991, became 15 independent states. The President of the USA and the President of Russia, the largest and most influential politically, militarily and economically, had expressed the hope in January 1992 to substantially reduce the expenditure on armaments and thus make the world a safer and securer place to live in.

The promise of cooperation between the Presidents of Russia and the USA is good sign for humanity as a whole and in normalizing the international relations in particular based upon mutual respect and peaceful coexistence. This has given a new hope to this troubled and divided world, and certainly it is 'nourishing' the UN system as well. The UN role in maintaining peace has increased through this cooperation of the former rivals. The UN may not be a place to provide a forum in which to conduct show-down business, as it has often been, but could be a fresh hope for lovers of peace and prosperity, which is centrally the hope of the inhabitants of this planet, (the goodwill and harmony among nations being based upon mutual respect, peaceful coexistence, and unconditional international cooperation).

With all this discussion, a serious question arises as to what does this entire mean to the people of Africa, Asia, and Latin America? Would there be a joint exploitation of these people who are still the victims of the colonialism due to their lack of economic independence? Will the poor nations be benefited from the growing cooperation between Russia and the USA, or will this be just a merger of two military powers?

As far as the record from 1950 to 1990 is concerned, has been proved quantitatively in the following chapter that the debt, aid and arms have not helped the economic development of the teeming millions in Africa, Asia, and USA. The late Prime Minister of Canada, Lester Pearson[4], said "The economic assistance has, at best, made little contribution to the aided nations' growth and, at most, has seriously distorted it." "...Trade and investment carried on between unequal partners do not produce sustained growth for the weaker party." This is clear from Chapter 2 of this book, because the total payments of interests and amortization caused serious deficit in the balance of payments, making even more acute the scarcity of foreign exchange. Similar statements, so far as the Third World and her development are concerned, have frequently been made by the governments of the Netherlands, the Scandinavian nations in general, and Sweden in particular, as well as the government of Switzerland.

In the aftermath of the death of communism in the former USSR, the pledge of cooperation between Russia and the USA is good and encouraging, but there is ground for suspicion by the poor nations. I am afraid the Third World nations tend to incline towards a greater feeling of fear and insecurity. I fear this could lead to a new cold war between the rich and the poor nations, regardless of their contradictory political structure, administrative institutions, and the socio-cultural value systems.

The theory and practice of non-alignment, the 'ism' of the underdeveloped nations, the so called Third World initiated by the late Prime Minister of India, J.L. Nehru, in 1950s, now and then gets a new momentum at the United Nations, and creates an environment that lays down the foundations for a new confrontation based on poverty and affluence of nations, and not on differing ideologies, and thus enhances the bitterness and frustration among the underdeveloped nations. There were many views and ideologies expressed by various leaders of the Third World. Many comment the investments from the developed nations' multinational corporations have emerged as a single factor to influence the host governments in the exercise of their sovereign rights and intervene in the functioning of their domestic affairs.

With the fall of communism in Eastern Europe, and economic unity of the entire European countries, I would like to raise some questions before I stress why entire Europe and the USA must come forward to help the poor nations to eradicate their poverty and provide necessary infrastructure for economic development. Who helped Europe to develop? Who helped the US to develop? First, the term 'developed' or 'underdeveloped' are related terms. Second, during the industrial revolution, the developed nations were exploiting the manpower and the natural resources of the three continents: Africa, Asia, and Latin America, the poorer parts of the earth today than under their colonial yoke. Did the developed nations of today not exploit the manpower, either as slave trade or the cheap labour? Did they pay fair prices for the natural resources of their colonies? These are the determinants that "developed the developed nations of today." Lester Pearson[5] said that, as a matter of fact, they (developed nations) borrowed extensively for which certainly not a single penny was paid in commercial return. On the other hand, when the underdeveloped nations of today receive aid and investment from the developed nations, they have to pay back many times more in commercial return. When the underdeveloped nations fail to pay back these enormous amounts of loans and investments, new loans are arranged to pay back the interests. In May 1963, George Thomson[6], then Minister for Foreign Affairs in the British Government, said that 28 per cent of the British 'aid' goes to pay back the interests on the former aid. No wonder, Lester Pearson[7] had to say, while speaking in a Conference on International Development in February 1970 in New York at Columbia University, "since aid, particularly tied aid, is in some measure simply a way of keeping the poorer community in a position of dependence on the aid giver, this tool perpetuates what is in essence a colonial relationship." The "cost of servicing the foreign public debts by the underdeveloped nations will rise from U.S. $5200 million in 1969 to U.S. $9200 million in 1977. The revenues (profits and interests) realized on private investment will surely rise $8000 million in 1977."[8] This means that the outflow of capital will exceed the total amount of capital receipts. This trend has been going on. There is still no sign of reversal. The poor countries are giving the rich countries much more than what they receive from them.

This is the irony of the present sophisticated and complicated economic system of the free market economies. The underdeveloped nations have now begun to calculate the amount of 'profits' from the 'losses' of 'aids' and 'investment'. The only way to get out of the 'network' of the free market economies is just to break away from them. If it does happen, wouldn't it lead to hostilities? The underdeveloped nations surely cannot be blamed for this tragedy, because the endurance of bitterness and frustrations has its limits. According to UN Economic Commission for Latin America, the US monopolies received in the period 1946-56, was $3.17 dollars for everyone dollar invested there. In the same period, profits amounting to $5600 million were shipped back to the US. In the fifteen years between 1947-62, the influx of new US investment in Latin America was $6500 million, but the profits pumped out[9] reached $10,000 million. In the present quarter of a century, wrote Kwame Nkrumah[10], the big American rubber firm, Firestone has taken $160 million worth of rubber out of Liberia. In return, the Liberian government has received a paltry sum of $8 million. The average net profit made by this American Company is three times the entire Liberian revenue. Kwame Nkrumah[11] said that the American aim is not just aid but part of foreign policy. The Committee calculated that 44 per cent of the American aid was military and economic support for allied countries bordering the communist block; and, if the sums spent in Vietnam and Laos are included, the share of the total appropriations comes to 72 per cent. Kwame Nkrumah[12] also stated that the methods of neo-colonialists are "subtle and varied". The neo-colonists "operate not only in the economic field, but also in the political, religious, ideological and cultural spheres." This statement clearly reflects how the people from underdeveloped nations are 'modernized,' while they receive training and/or education in a developed country.

Let us now turn towards Europe and the Third World. I would like to look at the EEC and its economic relation with the poor nations. Britain's entry into the EEC in 1973 began to affect the relations of Britain with the poor Commonwealth Asian nations. In 1977, a Generalized System of Preference (GSP) replaced the system of trade preference among all the Commonwealth members until then. Associate Membership had been offered to most Commonwealth States as well as to the Yaunde Group of former French colonies, but not to the Commonwealth countries of Asia: (i) India, (ii) Bangladesh, (iii) Sri Lanka (Ceylon), (iv) Malaysia, (v) Singapore, (vi) Hong Kong, and (vii) Pakistan.[13] According to the new deal that allows British entry into the enlarged EEC, these seven Commonwealth Asian nations[14] "will lose the Commonwealth preferences hitherto accorded them by Britain. Hong Kong and India, which together accounted for 60 per cent of the British imports from the Commonwealth Asia in 1970, both stand to lose a great deal from the phasing out of the remaining Commonwealth preferences in the British markets". Instead, the GSP[15] (Generalized System of Preferences) adopted by the EEC on January 1, 1974, governs the imports from all the non-associate countries.

In the light of the above discussion, it is imperative that the planning of the underdeveloped nations should not be based upon foreign aid, foreign capital, and foreign collaboration. If this is not done, the problem of hunger and poverty can never be solved. The exploitation of manpower in the form of cheap labour, and unfair prices paid for the natural resources of the underdeveloped nations by the developed market economies are the foundations on which the present system of international economical exploitation rests.

This unbalanced economy, the feelings of insecurity, the frustrated desires, and the well-planned exploitation of the economies of the underdeveloped nations, pose a serious threat to international peace and security. This will be a tragedy, unless there is a positive change in the attitudes of the developed nations regarding unconditional international cooperation among the nations within the framework of the UN Charter and the implementation of the resolutions/ agreements of the international conferences, especially CATT and UNCTAD. The undeveloped nations cannot be expected to remain as they are for an uncertain and indefinite period. But at present they certainly are going through this process of uncertainty. U Thant[16], in his capacity as the Secretary General of the UN in 1969, said,

> I can only conclude from the information available to me as the Secretary General that the members of the UN have perhaps ten years left in which to subordinate their ancient quarrels and launch a global partnership to curb the arms race, to improve the human environment, to defuse the population explosion...and to supply the required momentum to developmental efforts. If such global partnership is not forged within the next decade, then I very much fear that the problems that I have mentioned will have reached such a staggering proportion that they will be beyond our capacity to control.

Probably having this statement in mind and the lessons from the failures of the first UN Development Decade, in 1970, the UN International Development Strategy for the 1970s was launched. This strategy was based upon the then published (1969) Pearson Report on the terms of International Development and the UNCTAD-I and UNCTAD-II resolutions. Unfortunately, neither the recommendations made in the Pearson Report nor the UNCTAD resolutions have been carried out. This strategy was dead even before its scheduled midterm review in 1975. For the 1980s we have the Brandt[17] Commission Report and for the 1990s we have the South Commission Report. With all the discussion so far in this chapter, in terms of economic relations between developed and developing, the developing countries have been left with the following alternatives:

1. Let the present international monetary system and the monopoly of the developed market economies continue;
2. Cut themselves off from the above alternative and make 'profits' from 'losses' of 'aid' and 'investment' as discussed earlier, or
3. To make a clean break from the alternative No.1, and follow a rough course of 'go it alone; with the highest degree of bitterness and frustrations, the way the Chinese accomplished in the aftermath of Communist take-over, and practiced in Tanzania without success.

If the present international economic system were allowed to continue, the outflow of capital would exceed the total amount of capital receipts. Doing so, would keep the underdeveloped nations in the position of permanent parasite. In other words, the underdeveloped nations, who were earlier robbed mercilessly of their manpower and natural resources in colonial period, would keep that exploitation alive. Under the banner of 'aids', 'loans' from the developed returns and thus, this alternative leaves no option but to allow one to be exploited, like a featherless bird solely at the mercy of the hawk.

The second alternative is that the underdeveloped nations can cut themselves off from the present world economic system and the monopolies of the developed market economies, which is just a 'rich men's club'. This is clearly visible from the trade between rich and the poor nations and between rich and the rich nations. This alternative has a logic and can be justified analytically, since this 'loss' of 'aid' and 'investment' would at least be a 'gain' equivalent to what exceeds the capital inflow. If this alternative is opted, it will gravely endanger international peace and security and will eventually lead to war-like hostilities.

The reckless initiation of the nuclear warfare by any country, whether of World I, II, or III, will certainly blow this earth up many times over. The aftermath of this nuclear warfare may not see the human race, not even insect life, on this planet. Is this the consequence of our living in a 'civilized' era? At the time of Cuban Missile crisis in 1962, Jawaharlal Nehru did not speak of World War III, but he rather chose to say something about the World War IV. He said that the World War IV would be fought with bows and arrows. This means that he took the annihilation of this planet and its civilization for granted if World War had broken out in 1962. The bows and arrows he mentioned were probably of a new evolution of mankind in the aftermath of the nuclear warfare. In May 1972, when the United States mined the ports of Vietnam, there was a growing speculation that the other superpower, the USSR, might sweep out the mines. This could, if it had occurred, lead to a nuclear confrontation. The Canadian Prime Minister, P.E. Trudeau, hoped that the war would not break out. He further stated that if war broke out, "you" (the audience) wouldn't be around anywhere to blame "me", clearly meaning we all would be dead. Thus the consequences of the second alternative, that the underdeveloped nations cut themselves off from the present international monetary system and the monopolies of the free market economies, would be a very serious blow to international peace and security and could lead to a serious conflict between the family of nations, not to mention the possibilities of nuclear confrontation. Such is the civilization of this age, which is known as 'modern' on a comparative basis with the earlier civilizations. As a matter of fact, this 'modern' civilization is a barbaric civilization where more than two-thirds of the people on earth struggle for food and shelter and cannot get them. In the earlier civilizations, it was seldom like that. Is not it shameful to call our civilization of the present a 'modern civilization'? The consequences of this second alternative are thus very serious, and this is not a practical solution if we want this world to go on, and not leave it dormant like the satellite moon of the planet earth.

The third alternative is to make a clean break from the

present world economic system and the monopolies of the developed market economies and to follow a rough course, 'go it alone', the way the Chinese managed in the aftermath of Communist take-over in 1949, under Mao. Not all the underdeveloped nations have enough resources and the capabilities to opt for this alternative. The Chinese in the subsequent years (in the 1960s) virtually had no relations with the rest of the world. They developed nuclear warfare machinery. They did not produce the consumer goods required by their people. The decade of isolation of the sixties saw the new decade of the 1970s when the nations around the world realized the Chinese madness. By madness, I mean the Chinese threat of nuclear warfare. The rest of the world created a new social 'courtesy' of how to shake hands with a clenched fist. All these nuclear development for war and weaponry were accomplished at the same time when the "Cultural Revolution" was going on within the nation. To rid China of so much western influence on native soil, a "cultural revolution" was required in a country which has one of the oldest recorded history of culture and civilization. This third alternative does not provide an acceptable solution on which to build the economic relations between the rich and poor nations.

None of the above three alternatives provide any practical solution based on international friendship. It is clear from this discussion that we in this world, at this point in history, are in a very critical situation. One solution is still possible, if we could foresee beyond our own narrow, selfish interests. And that is: with the death of communism in Eastern Europe, and the emerging economic unity within all countries of Europe, the united Europe and the USA should come forward to help the developing countries, keeping in mind mutual respect, unconditional international co-operation, and peaceful coexistence among the nations within the framework of the UN Charter. Now that the period of cold war has been practically consigned to the books of history, there is bound to be drastic cut in the military budget of all countries in the world, $1000 billion a year is now being spent on arms production, as reported by the World Bank in its 1991 annual report, entitled 'The World Development Report, 1991'. Out of this $1000 billion expenditure on arms, the developed countries and 20 per cent spend 80 per cent by the developing countries. The developed countries should now invest a substantial portion of these cuts in their military expenditures on the economic development of the developing countries. It is the moral duty of the developed countries for, as the late Dr. Martin Luther King[18], Jr. said:

> We in the West must bear in mind that the poor countries are poor primarily because we have exploited them through political or economic colonialism.

To accomplish the economic development of developing countries, based upon mutual trust among the nations, we have to redefine our existing definition of aids, loans, and private investment in such a way that they make a positive contribution to the development system of the underdeveloped nations. This would mean that the poor nations have to be assured of a new faith in the developed nations. Unless this assurance is practiced, beyond its current tones, the underdeveloped must stop the plunder that goes on in the name of "charity".

While celebrating the death of Communism in the former USSR and Eastern European countries, the President of USA, George Bush[19], in his State of the Union message to the US Congress for 1991 proudly proclaimed:

> Communism died this year. By the grace of God, America won the cold war. We are the United States of America, the leader of the West that has become the leader of the World.

Despite this declaration by the President of USA, the fact is that for USA, the leader of the West, to become the leader of the world, the economic developmental projects for the upliftment of the teeming millions in the Third World will have to be financed by USA along with Western countries. This approach towards the financing of developmental projects in the developing countries may be on the lines recommended in 1980 by no less a person than Willy Brandt[20], the Nobel prize winner for Peace and former Chancellor of the then West Germany:

> There must be a substantial increase in the transfer of resources to developing countries in order to finance:
>
> 1. Projects and programmes to alleviate poverty and to expand food production, especially in the least developed countries.
> 2. Exploration and development of energy and mineral resources.
> 3. Stabilization of the prices and earnings of commodity exports and expanded domestic processing of commodities.

In the absence of such finance for the development projects of the developing countries, as recommended by Willy Brandt, USA can hardly aspire to become the genuine leader of the teeming millions in the Third World. However, to become a self-proclaimed leader of the World by the brute force of formidable military machine that USA is is a different matter.

## NOTES

1. Martin Luther King, Jr., *Conscience for Change*, The Canadian Broadcasting Corporation, Toronto; 1967, p. 36.
2. *Ibid.*
3. L.B. Pearson, Partners in Development (New York: Praeger Pub., 1969); p. 8.
4. Lester Pearson, "Pearson on Pearson Report", *CERES Magazine*, FAO of the U.N., Rome, Italy; March-April, 1979; p. 20.
5. Lester Pearson, "Pearson on Pearson Report", *op. cit.*, p. 22.
6. Quoted in Jack Woddis, *Introduction to Neo-Colonialism* (New York: International Pub., 1971); p. 91.
7. L.B. Pearson, "Pearson on Pearson Report", *op. cit.*, p. 24.
8. A. Angelopoulos, "Who Aids Whom", in *CERES Magazine*, FAO the United Nations, Rome, Italy, Nov.- Dec., 1971; p. 48.
9. Jack Woddis, *Introduction to Neo-Colonialism* (New York: International Pub., 1971); p. 49.
10. Quoted in *Ibid.*, p. 90.
11. *Ibid.*, p. 96.

12. *Ibid.*, p. 6.
13. Pakistan retained her commercial links with Commonwealth, despite her resignation from it, after the war of 1971 with India that gave birth to Bangladesh, formerly East Pakistan.
14. See Peter Tulloch, *The Seven Outside: Commonwealth Asia's Trade with the Enlarged EEC*, (London: Overseas Development Institute, 1974); p. 25.
15. The volume of G.S.P. in measured, as the value of imports including C.I.F. (cost, interest and freight charge) multiplied by the per cent rate of preference. A similar formula is used for measuring the values of preferences gained through G.S.P. access to Britain and other six. The other six are the original members of the EEC. *See* Peter Tulloch, *Ibid.*, p. 4.
16. Quoted in *The Challenge of a Decade: Global Development or Breakdown*, (New York: United Nations, 1971); p. 1.
17. *North-South: A Programme for Survival* (Cambridge, Mass.: The MIT Pr. 1980). The report of the Independent Commission on International Development Issues under the chairmanship of Willy Brandt, former West German Chancellor.
18. Martin Luther King, Jr., *Conscience for Change*, (Canadian Broadcasting Corporation, Toronto,1967); p. 36.
19. *Times of India*, New Delhi; 30-1-1992; p. 1.
20. *North-South: A Programme for Survival* (Cambridge: The MIT Press, 1980); p. 290.

# 2

# Foreign Debt and Aid

*The upshot is that debt has become a form of bondage, and the indebted economies have become indentured economies—a clear manifestation of neo-colonialism.*

*—Julius K. Nyerere[1], 1990*
*The South Commission Report*

*...I do not know of any country in the world that might have become prosperous with the help and formulae of the International Monetary Fund (IMF).*

*—Kuldip Nayar[2], 1991*

*For every $1 the West gives in aid to the developing countries, $9 comes back in debt service.*

*—Ash Narain Roy[3], 2000*

## A. FOREIGN DEBT AND AID: THE SITUATION DURING 1950-1970

Let us look at the financial resources of developed and the developing countries, and the gap between the two. Fig. 2.1 shows that 34 per cent of the total population controlled 87.5 per cent of the total wealth between 1950 and 1970.[4] Table 2.1 shows how the remaining 66 per cent of the total population, the underdeveloped, share this remaining 12.5 per cent of the total wealth. The enormous increase in the wealth-producing capacity is due to the development of science and technology and the industrial revolution approximately between the years 1850 and 1950. During this period, the liberated nations of today were under colonial rule and thus could not benefit from the industrial revolution.

Today, every nation depends directly or indirectly upon another nation or nations, and this gap (Fig. 2.1) naturally creates a desire to rise and make its life better. The developed nations did, however, realize this, and so the idea developed of international development aids and cooperation in the form of loans, grants, private investments, technical assistance and technical know-how, etc., enabling these liberated and low developed nations to help themselves in their economic take-off period and towards the self-sustained economic growth. A.M. Dambe[5] rightly said that "We do not regard it as our right to be helped, we do not demand handouts, but we welcome the generosity of our friends who are trying to help us to stand on our own feet."

An account follows of development assistance from developed nations, international bodies, bilateral assistance, and its nature, purpose and scope. After the Second World War, no attention was directed towards the underdeveloped nations. In the 1950s, the development assistance was almost 100 per cent in grants. In the 1960s, it sank to 50 per cent. Both aids and loans were tied to export from the donor nations, thus depriving the rights of the underdeveloped nations to invite international competition and thus forcing them to pay relatively high price, or monopoly prices of the standards set by the donor nations. Table 2.2 shows the net flow of financial resources from DAC member nations received by the developing countries, during 1961-71 period. This net flow is defined as a gross disbursement *minus* amortization of the principal. We see from this figure that percentages of grants, or grants-like, have been continuously declining from 47 per cent in 1962 to 21 per cent in 1971 but the assistance from the multilateral resources has been varying between 9, 10, or 11 per cent.

Table 2.3 shows the net flow of financial resources from multilateral agencies to developing nations, a continuous trend in increase over the whole decade. This is certainly a good sign of the real work towards increasing international cooperation to provide development assistance from multilateral agencies, though it is only an approximate 10 per cent of the total development assistance provided by the developed nations;

the rest of the developed nations handle by themselves on bilateral basis. The aid from multilateral agencies enables the recipient nation to buy a product from the international competitive market. The bilateral aid is usually tied up to buy only from the specific donor, sometimes even at a much higher price, or to fulfill the undue political interests, or to bargain on conditions totally unfavorable to the recipient nation.

**Table 2.1:** Selected Less Developed Countries by Growth in Gross National Product and Level of Per Capita Income [GNP Per Capita (1967)]

| *GNP Growth Rate, Annual Average (1960-67)* | *Under $ 100* | *$ 100 to under $ 200* | *$ 200 to under $ 300* | *$ 300 to under $ 500* | *$ 500 and more* | *No. of Countries* |
|---|---|---|---|---|---|---|
| Above 6% | | South Korea<br>Mauritania<br>Thailand | El Salvador<br>Iran<br>Ivory Coast<br>Jordan<br>China (Taiwan) | Nicaragua<br>Peru | Cyprus<br>Greece<br>Israel<br>Libya<br>Mexico<br>Panama<br>Spain<br>Trinidad & Tobago<br>Yugoslavia | 19 |
| 5-6% | Guinea<br>Malawi<br>Pakistan | Bolivia<br>Syria<br>U.A.R. | Honduras<br>Iraq<br>Malaysia<br>Papua & New Guinea<br>Turkey | Costa Rica<br>Guatemala | | 13 |
| 4-5% | Ethiopia<br>Tanzania | Ecuador<br>Kenya<br>Philippines<br>Zambia | Brazil<br>Colombia<br>Paraguay | Gabon | Chile<br>Lebanon<br>Venezuela | 13 |
| 3-4% | India<br>Nigeria | Ceylon<br>Congo (B)<br>Morocco<br>Sudan<br>Uganda | Dominican Republic<br>Ghana<br>Liberia<br>Tunisia | Guyana<br>Jamaica<br>Ghana | | 13 |
| Below 3% | Burma<br>Congo (K)<br>Haiti<br>Mali<br>Somalia | Cameroon<br>Indonesia | Algeria<br>Senegal | | Argentina<br>Uruguay | 11 |

*Source:* Lester B. Pearson, *Partners in Development* (New York: Praeger Pub. 1969), p. 360.

**Table 2.2:** Net Flow of Financial Resources Received by Developing Countries by Source, 1961-1971

*(USS Millions)*

| | *1961* | *1962* | *1963* | *1964* | *1965* | *1966* | *1967* | *1968* | *1969* | *1970* | *1971* |
|---|---|---|---|---|---|---|---|---|---|---|---|
| DAC Grants | 3991 | 4020 | 3942 | 3806 | 3714 | 3701 | 3578 | 3344 | 3250 | 3355 | 3681 |
| DAC Bilateral Official Loans | 21401 | 1438 | 1711 | 1713 | 2132 | 2341 | 2726 | 3031 | 2909 | 3265 | 3760 |
| Other Bilateral | 222 | 307 | 388 | 445 | 432 | 340 | 370 | 375 | 475 | 550 | 550 |
| Total Bilateral Official | 5614 | 5765 | 6041 | 5964 | 6278 | 6382 | 6674 | 6750 | 6634 | 7170 | 7991 |
| Multilateral | 230 | 481 | 712 | 836 | 972 | 1106 | 1205 | 1151 | 1358 | 1490 | 1882 |
| Total Official | 35844 | 6246 | 6753 | 6800 | 7250 | 7488 | 7879 | 7901 | 7992 | 8660 | 9873 |
| DAC Bilateral Private | 3016 | 2214 | 2590 | 3268 | 3874 | 3783 | 3912 | 5613 | 6168 | 6506 | 7560 |
| Total Receipts | 8860 | 8460 | 9343 | 10068 | 11124 | 11271 | 11791 | 13514 | 14160 | 15166 | 17433 |
| 1 (Percent of total) | | | | | | | | | | | |
| DAC Grants 1 | 45 | 47 | 42 | 38 | 33 | 33 | 30 | 25 | 23 | 22 | 21 |
| DAC Bilateral Official Loans 2 | 16 | 17 | 18 | 17 | 19 | 21 | 23 | 22 | 21 | 22 | 22 |
| Other Bilateral | 2 | 4 | 4 | 4 | 4 | 3 | 3 | 3 | 3 | 4 | 3 |

*(Contd.)*

(*Contd.*)

| | *1961* | *1962* | *1963* | *1964* | *1965* | *1966* | *1967* | *1968* | *1969* | *1970* | *1971* |
|---|---|---|---|---|---|---|---|---|---|---|---|
| Total Bilateral Official | 63 | 68 | 64 | 59 | 56 | 57 | 57 | 50 | 47 | 47 | 46 |
| Multilateral | 3 | 6 | 8 | 8 | 9 | 10 | 10 | 9 | 9 | 10 | 11 |
| Total Official 3 | 66 | 74 | 72 | 67 | 65 | 66 | 67 | 59 | 56 | 57 | 57 |
| DAC Bilateral Private 4 | 34 | 26 | 28 | 33 | 35 | 34 | 33 | 41 | 44 | 43 | 43 |
| Total Receipts | 100 | 100 | 100 | 100 | 100 | 100 | 100 | 100 | 100 | 100 | 100 |

*Note:* "Net Flow" as used in Table 3.1 through 3.4 is defined as gross disbursements *minus* amortization of principal.

1. Including "grant like" contributions.
2. Including rough estimates of flows from centrally planned economies.
3. Excluding grants by private voluntary agencies.
4. Dental may not add to totals due to rounding.

*Source:* Trends in developing countries, World Bank, Washington D.C., 1973; Table 4.1.

**Table 2.3:** Net Flow of Financial Resources from Multilateral Agencies to Developing Countries, 1961-1971

*(US$ millions)*

| | *1961* | *1962* | *1963* | *1964* | *1965* | *1966* | *1967* | *1968* | *1969* | *1970* | *1971*[3] |
|---|---|---|---|---|---|---|---|---|---|---|---|
| IDA | 1 | 25 | 105 | 148 | 277 | 272 | 368 | 215 | 250 | 162 | 288 |
| World Bank | 198 | 271 | 317 | 302 | 294 | 359 | 331 | 370 | 388 | 508 | 689 |
| IFC | 8 | 15 | 8 | 10 | 11 | 24 | 19 | 21 | 53 | 68 | 56 |
| Total Bank Group[1] | 207 | 311 | 430 | 460 | 582 | 655 | 718 | 606 | 691 | 738 | 1033 |
| Inter-American Development Bank | 7 | 59 | 140 | 192 | 170 | 186 | 203 | 230 | 312 | 341 | 361 |
| Asian Development Bank | - | - | - | - | - | - | - | 1 | 7 | 16 | 74 |
| African Development Bank | - | - | - | - | - | - | - | - | 1 | 3 | 10 |
| European Development Fund | 16 | 53 | 65 | 90 | 115 | 140 | 143 | 149 | 159 | 182 | 180 |
| UNDP[2] | - | 58 | 77 | 94 | 105 | 125 | 141 | 165 | 187 | 210 | 224 |
| Grand Total | 230 | 481 | 712 | 836 | 972 | 1106 | 1205 | 1151 | 1358 | 1490 | 1882 |

1. For consistency with DAC listing of the developing countries, only loans to IDA Part II countries are included.
2. UNDP programme costs in projects: there are no repayments on UNDP assistance.
3. 1971 figures are provisional.

*Source*: Trends in Developing Countries, World Bank, Washington D.C., 1973; Table 4.5.

The World Bank, charges interest, but provides assistance or without any political leverage to any nation involved. However, at the crucial period of the nationalization of the Suez Canal, the World Bank simply did not finance the Aswan dam project in UAR, mainly because of political pressures from the Governments of France and British. This project was later financed by the Soviets. This type of example stains these bodies whose very purpose is to develop the underdeveloped solely on moral and humanitarian grounds. These multilateral agencies should be kept free from such repetition of undue political leverage.

The development loans, private investments, export credits, and other public outlays involve heavy indebtedness and service payments and substantial amounts of interest to be borne by the underdeveloped nations which, on unfavorable terms, becomes a heavy debt to repay, especially until the self-sustained economy, which is but a dream at least for some time to come, is reached.

Now let us review Tables 2.4, 2.5 and 2.6. We can see that every nation and every region in the developing areas is burdening her with external debt. Every year they owe more

**Table 2.4:** Developing Countries Outstanding Debts at the End of 1969

| | | | |
|---|---|---|---|
| 1. | Public and publicly guaranteed debts | – | US $ 60 billion* |
| 2. | Private debt | | US $ 30 billion** |
| | Total | – | US $ 90 billion |

* According to the World Bank (Annual Report, 1970, pp. 57) external public debt, which had already doubled at the end of 1964, totalled U.S. $53.4 billion in 1968. On the basis of the preliminary estimates of the World Bank, by the end of 1969 the total external public debt reached the $60 billion figure approximately.

** According to OECD, private investment and lending totalled approximately U.S. $30 billion in 1966 with as much as $14.5 billion representing direct investment in oil production and other minerals.

*Source:* The Third World and the Rich Countries, Angelo Angelopolous, p. 118, Praeger, New York, 1972.

**Table 2.5:** External Public Debt Outstanding of Selected Countries as on December 31, 1965-1970

*(US$ millions)*

| | *1965* | *1966* | *1967* | *1968* | *1969* | *1970* |
|---|---|---|---|---|---|---|
| India[1] | 6055.7 | 7123.2 | 7425.6 | 8277.1 | 8694.6 | 9235.1 |
| Pakistan | 2095.4 | 2601.6 | 2965.5 | 3331.5 | 3788.7 | 4302.1 |
| Brazil[2] | 3051.0 | 3201.0 | 3250.8 | 3495.7 | 3522.2 | 3808.5 |
| Mexico | 2138.8 | 2301.0 | 2671.6 | 3126.3 | 3441.3 | 3791.2 |
| Indonesia | 2100.0 | 2087.8 | 2263.7 | 2560.9 | 2984.2 | 3462.8 |
| Iran | 824.1 | 987.8 | 1398.6 | 1740.4 | 2312.3 | 3021.5 |
| Korea, Republic of | 371.0 | 685.3 | 1251.4 | 1750.5 | 2326.3 | 2636.8 |
| Turkey | 1323.6 | 1535.0 | 1780.0 | 1970.4 | 2308.0 | 2626.1 |
| Chile | 1118.7 | 1325.7 | 1881.4 | 2027.6 | 2179.2 | 2503.4 |
| Argentina | 1967.7 | 1924.9 | 2061.3 | 2207.2 | 2355.7 | 2457.3 |
| Israel | 905.2 | 1003.2 | 1350.8 | 1648.9 | 1714.5 | 2022.2 |
| Yugoslavia | 1746.2 | 1685.7 | 1802.6 | 1748.3 | 1715.7 | 1729.5 |
| Colombia | 994.6 | 1016.6 | 1160.7 | 1320.8 | 1550.2 | 1720.4 |
| Spain | 454.5 | 515.5 | 949.2 | 1208.0 | 1479.5 | 1530.0 |
| Peru | 690.1 | 912.0 | 1001.0 | 1101.2 | 1115.1 | 1184.4 |
| Greece | 515.1 | 536.1 | 536.4 | 620.0 | 788.6 | 1003.6 |
| Total, above countries (As % of total external public debt, 80 developing countries) | 70.4 | 70.0 | 69.9 | 70.2 | 70.3 | 70.5 |

1. Estimated on the basis of incomplete data. Fiscal years beginning from April 1.
2. Includes some non-guaranteed debt of the private sector to suppliers and excludes the undisguised portion of suppliers credits and of bilateral official loans except for those owed to the US government. Also excludes financial credits, mostly to the private sector.
3. Estimated on the basis of Central Bank data.

*Source*: Trends in developing countries, World Bank (I.B.R.D.), Washington D.C., 1973, Table 4.6.

**Table 2.6:** External Public Debt Outstanding and Debt Service Payments as on December 31, 1965-1970

*(US$ millions)*

| | *1965* | *1966* | *1967* | *1968* | *1969* | *1970* |
|---|---|---|---|---|---|---|
| *Africa* | | | | | | |
| Debt outstanding | 6148.8 | 7202.2 | 8181.0 | 9018.6 | 9688.0 | 10693.5 |
| Service payments | 467.2 | 477.4 | 463.9 | 494.7 | 688.0 | 798.7 |
| *East Asia* | | | | | | |
| Debt outstanding | 3895.4 | 4347.7 | 5289.7 | 6295.4 | 7776.4 | 9195.3 |
| Service payments | 193.7 | 225.3 | 259.4 | 286.1 | 386.9 | 614.2 |
| *Middle East* | | | | | | |
| Debt outstanding | 2178.9 | 2514.0 | 3677.9 | 4364.4 | 5017.8 | 5732.8 |
| Service payments | 388.7 | 468.0 | 560.7 | 595.0 | 688.9 | 746.4 |
| *South Asia* | | | | | | |
| Debt outstanding | 8843.7 | 10517.5 | 11294.9 | 12666.4 | 13653.6 | 14741.6 |
| Service payments | 267.3 | 286.4 | 229.6 | 334.3 | 451.6 | 479.3 |
| *Southern Europe* | | | | | | |
| Debt outstanding | 4096.5 | 4324.4 | 5115.8 | 5601.0 | 6367.5 | 6963.2 |
| Service payments | 439.0 | 446.7 | 443.0 | 502.6 | 541.9 | 701.8 |
| *Western Hemisphere* | | | | | | |
| Debt outstanding | 12228.1 | 13181.0 | 14743.1 | 16368.9 | 17671.0 | 19372.1 |
| Service payments | 1721.3 | 1927.4 | 2058.0 | 2210.9 | 2246.4 | 2560.0 |
| *Total 80 Developing Countries* | | | | | | |
| Debt outstanding | 37402.4 | 42086.8 | 48302.5 | 54314.6 | 60174.1 | 66698.5 |
| Service payments | 3477.1 | 3831.2 | 4014.6 | 4423.6 | 5003.5 | 5900.3 |

*Source*: Trends in Developing Countries, World Bank (I.B.R.D.), Washington DC, 1973, Table 4.5.

money and pay more service payments than the preceding year. Where service payments are concerned, Africa's are nearly equal between 1965-70. On an annual average, there is a sharp decrease in the Middle East from 12.26 per cent to 8.36 per cent, because the Middle Eastern nations earn a comparatively larger amount of foreign exchange by exporting oil than other nations in the developing regions. The service payments of East Asia and South Asia have risen from 4.97 per cent to 6.67 per cent, and from 4.39 per cent to 5.06 per cent, respectively, of their outstanding debts during the same period.

Table 2.7 gives the GNP per capita of the developing regions, during the 1960-70 period Table 2.8 gives the same in selected developing countries, and Table 2.9 gives the total amount of payments of amortization and interests by the developing nations. When I look at these figures of so little GNP and the large amounts of amortization and interests for outstanding debts, I have no doubt that if this trend continues, the underdeveloped can never be able to achieve economic independence. To me, the political independence that was achieved by struggling for centuries is of no use unless economic independence is found as well. J.K. Nyerere[6] says that:

> "To burden the people with big loans, the repayment of which will be beyond their means, is not to help them but to make them suffer. ...It would be more appropriate for us to spend time in the villages[7] showing the people how to bring about development through their own efforts rather than going on so many long and expensive journeys abroad in search of development money."

The problem is that how the underdeveloped nations can be their own masters ? How to achieve economic independence[7] after having been politically independent from the colonial rulers? To help reduce interest and amortization burden, it is necessary to implement the recommendation made in Pearson Report[8], which said that "the terms of all official development assistance loans should henceforth provide for interest of no more than 2 per cent, a maturity of 25 and 40 years, and a grace period of 7 to 10 years." The present bank loans are usually with a maturity of 15 of 25 years, and at an interest rate on the average of 6.0 to 6.5 per cent. The IDA loans are payable in 50 years and carry a service charge of 0.75 per cent.[9]

**Table 2.7:** Gross National Product Per Capita by Regions, 1960 and 1970

*(1970 US$)*

| *Regions* | *Countries Included* | *GNP per capita* | |
|---|---|---|---|
| | | *1960* | *1970* |
| Developing Regions | 79 | 185 | 250 |
| Africa | 31 | 145 | 180 |
| Asia | 14 | 100 | 125 |
| Middle East | 6 | 285 | 460 |
| Latin America | 21 | 435 | 560 |
| Southern Europe | 7 | 430 | 695 |
| Developed Regions | 21 | 2010 | 2750 |
| Japan | 1 | 750 | 1920 |
| North America | 2 | 3820 | 4660 |
| Europe, excluding Southern | 15 | 1775 | 2575 |
| USSR | 1 | 1160 | 1790 |
| Australia and New Zealand | 2 | 2090 | 2800 |

*Source:* Trends in Developing Countries, World Bank, Washington DC, 1973; Table 2.5.

**Table 2.8:** Gross National Product Per Capita, Selected Developing Countries and Years, 1950-1970

*(1970 US$)*

| *Countries* | *1950* | *1955* | *1960* | *1965* | *1970* |
|---|---|---|---|---|---|
| *Africa* | | | | | |
| Cameroon | 130 | 130 | 125 | 150 | 180 |
| Ghana | 205 | 250 | 310 | 315 | 310 |
| Malawi | 65 | 60 | 65 | 70 | 80 |
| Nigeria | 85 | 100 | 105 | 110 | 120 |
| Uganda | 95 | 95 | 110 | 115 | 130 |
| Zambia | 180 | 190 | 240 | 305 | 400 |
| Zaire | 60 | 70 | 75 | 70 | 90 |
| *Asia* | | | | | |
| Burma | 50 | 60 | 75 | 80 | 80 |

*(Contd.)*

*(Contd.)*

*(1970 US$)*

| *Countries* | *1950* | *1955* | *1960* | *1965* | *1970* |
|---|---|---|---|---|---|
| India | 75 | 85 | 95 | 100 | 110 |
| Korea, Republic of | 100 | 125 | 135 | 160 | 250 |
| Malaysia | 245 | 265 | 280 | 320 | 380 |
| Pakistan–Bangladesh | 70 | 70 | 75 | 85 | 100 |
| Philippines | 115 | 145 | 160 | 175 | 210 |
| *Latin America* | | | | | |
| Bolivia | 180 | 165 | 145 | 165 | 180 |
| Brazil | 215 | 260 | 310 | 335 | 420 |
| Chile | 560 | 565 | 605 | 675 | 720 |
| Columbia | 250 | 295 | 290 | 305 | 340 |
| Haiti | 110 | 110 | 115 | 110 | 110 |
| Mexico | 380 | 460 | 475 | 560 | 670 |
| Venezuela | 500 | 630 | 780 | 935 | 980 |
| *Europe, Middle East and North Africa* | | | | | |
| Egypt | 180 | 175 | 195 | 230 | 210 |
| Greece | 360 | 460 | 565 | 810 | 1090 |
| Israel | 750 | 960 | 1200 | 1595 | 1960 |
| Morocco | 225 | 245 | 210 | 210 | 230 |
| Spain | 330 | 490 | 550 | 790 | 1020 |
| Turkey | 170 | 200 | 230 | 270 | 310 |

*Note*: 1. Rounded to nearest five dollars.

*Source:* Trends in Developing Countries, World Bank (I.B.R.D.), Washington DC, 1973; Table 2.6.

**Table 2.9:** The Total Payments of Amortization and Interests

| *Year* | *US$ million* |
|---|---|
| 1956 | 9.6 |
| 1957 | 11.0 |
| 1958 | 14.5 |
| 1959 | 44.4 |
| 1960 | 88.0 |
| 1961 | 214.4 |
| 1962 | 188.0 |
| 1963 | 198.6 |
| 1964 | 326.2 |
| 1965 | 268.6 |
| 1966 | 319.3 |
| 1967 | 368.0 |
| 1968 | 411.2 |

*Source:* L.B. Pearson, *Partners in Development*, Praeger Pub., New York, 1969, p. 299. This is the report submitted by the Rt. Hon. Pearson to the World Bank on International Development Issues.

It is preferable, however, to solve this problem in a different way, without putting any pressure on any developed nation for grants and loans, through 'Trade and Private Investment', which would be beneficial to both the developed and the underdeveloped, and would eventually lead towards economic independence.

## Trade and Private Investments

Tables 2.10 and 2.11 give the net flow of official development assistance and total net flows of financial resources (including private), respectively. The difference between the two tables gives the amount of private investments which has been shown graphically in Fig. 2.1. This figure shows that grants and grant-like portions of the development aids are on continuous decline: on the annual average it was 51.9 per cent, 45.4 per cent, 36.4 per cent and 32.9 per cent in 1960-62, 1963-65, 1965-68, and in 1969, respectively. During the same period, private investments have been increasing from 27.1 per cent, 27.9 per cent, 29.6 per cent and 32.4 per cent, respectively. Why is there decline in grants and continuous trend in increasing private investments? Most Western economists believe that private foreign capital investment[10] is in the interests of the investors, without considering much of the interests of the underdeveloped. Directly or indirectly, the United States is paying close to 90 per cent of the capital grants and technical assistance in various forms to the poor majority of the mankind. The rich countries, and in particular the United States, Gunnar Myrdal[11] points out, have acted upon the "double standard morality", insisting upon following a projectionist policy on their own behalf, while preaching the virtues of free trade to the underdeveloped world.

| *Population* | |
|---|---|
| Developed World 31% | Less Developed World 66 per cent |
| *Gross National Product* | |
| Developed World 87.5% | Less Developed World 12.5 per cent |

*Source:* Lester B. Pearson, Partners in Development, Praeger Pub., New York, 1969, p. 24.

**Fig. 2.1:** Population and Gross National Product

**Table 2.10:** Flow of Official Development Assistance

| | *Per capita GNP 1970* | | | *1966* | *1967* | *1968* | *1969* | *1970 (Premil.)* |
|---|---|---|---|---|---|---|---|---|
| | SUS | RANK | | | | | | |
| *(1)* | *(2)* | *(3)* | *(4)* | *(5)* | *(6)* | *(7)* | *(8)* | *(9)* |
| United States | 4770 | 1 | A | 3459 | 3567 | 3303 | 3092 | 3050 |
| | | | B | 45 | 44 | 38 | 33 | 31 |
| | | | C | 5-6 | 6-7 | 8 | 11 | 12 |
| Sweden | 3900 | 2 | A | 57 | 60 | 71 | 121 | 117 |
| | | | B | 26 | 25 | 28 | 43 | 37 |
| | | | C | 12 | 11 | 10 | 6 | 8-9 |
| Canada | 3780 | 3 | A | 187 | 198 | 175 | 245 | 346 |
| | | | B | 35 | 34 | 28 | 34 | 43 |
| | | | C | 9 | 9 | 11 | 10 | 6 |
| Switzerland | 3240 | 4 | A | 14 | 12 | 23 | 30 | 29 |
| | | | B | 10 | 07 | 13 | 16 | 14 |
| | | | C | 16 | 16 | 15 | 15 | 15 |
| Denmark | 3170 | 5 | A | 21 | 26 | 29 | 54 | 59 |
| | | | B | 19 | 21 | 23 | 39 | 38 |
| | | | C | 13 | 14 | 13 | 7 | 7 |
| Germany | 3010 | 6 | A | 440 | 528 | 553 | 579 | 599 |
| | | | B | 37 | 43 | 41 | 38 | 32 |
| | | | C | 8 | 8 | 6 | 8 | 11 |
| Norway | 2890 | 7 | A | 14 | 15 | 27 | 30 | 37 |
| | | | B | 18 | 17 | 29 | 30 | 33 |
| | | | C | 14 | 15 | 9 | 12 | 10 |
| France | 2870 | 8 | A | 745 | 826 | 874 | 955 | 951 |
| | | | B | 69 | 71 | 71 | 68 | 65 |
| | | | C | 1 | 2 | 1 | 2 | 1 |

(*Contd.*)

(Contd.)

| (1) | (2) | (3) | (4) | (5) | (6) | (7) | (8) | (9) |
|---|---|---|---|---|---|---|---|---|
| Australia | 2740 | 9 | A | 1246 | 157 | 160 | 175 | 208 |
| | | | B | 53 | 60 | 57 | 56 | 59 |
| | | | C | 3 | 3 | 3 | 3 | 3 |
| Belgium | 2600 | 10 | A | 76 | 89 | 88 | 116 | 120 |
| | | | B | 42 | 45 | 42 | 51 | 48 |
| | | | C | 7 | 5 | 5 | 5 | 4 |
| Netherlands | 2110 | 11 | A | 94 | 114 | 134 | 143 | 198 |
| | | | B | 45 | 49 | 53 | 51 | 63 |
| | | | C | 5-6 | 4 | 4 | 4 | 2 |
| United Kingdom | 1980 | 12 | A | 486 | 485 | 413 | 431 | 447 |
| | | | B | 46 | 44 | 40 | 39 | 37 |
| | | | C | 4 | 6-7 | 7 | 9 | 8-9 |
| Australia | 1690 | 13 | A | 31 | 26 | 23 | 15 | 19 |
| | | | B | 31 | 24 | 20 | 12 | 13 |
| | | | C | 10 | 12 | 14 | 16 | 16 |
| Japan | 1630 | 14 | A | 283 | 384 | 356 | 436 | 458 |
| | | | B | 28 | 32 | 25 | 26 | 23 |
| | | | C | 11 | 10 | 12 | 13 | 13 |
| Italy | 1520 | 15 | A | 78 | 155 | 146 | 130 | 142 |
| | | | B | 12 | 22 | 19 | 16 | 16 |
| | | | C | 15 | 13 | 15 | 14 | 14 |
| Portugal | 580 | 16 | A | 24 | 47 | 35 | 58 | 29 |
| | | | B | 59 | 1.02 | 0.69 | 1.02 | 0.45 |
| | | | C | 2 | 1 | 2 | 1 | 5 |

A Net Flows (US$ millions)
B Flow as percentage of GNP US dollars
C Rank of Members Based on Flow as percentage of GNP

*Source*: Canadian International Development Agency, Annual Review, Ottawa, Canada, 1971-72, p. 79.

**Table 2.11:** Total Net Flow of Financial Resources (including Private) from DAC Member Countries to Less Developed Countries and Multilateral Agencies, 1966-70

| | | *1966* | *1967* | *1968* | *1969* | *1970 (Prelim.)* |
|---|---|---|---|---|---|---|
| United States | A | 4884 | 5644 | 5723 | 4716 | .5971 |
| | B | .64 | .70 | .65 | .50 | .61 |
| | C | 9 | 9 | 12-13-14 | 15-16 | 15 |
| Sweden | A | 108 | 121 | 128 | 212 | 229 |
| | B | .48 | .50 | .50 | .75 | .73 |
| | C | 13 | 11 | 15 | 11 | 11 |
| Canada | A | 267 | 272 | 308 | 364 | 626 |
| | B | .47 | .45 | .46 | .50 | .77 |
| | C | 14 | 12 | 16 | 15-16 | 10 |
| Switzerland | A | 110 | 136 | 242 | 119 | 137 |
| | B | .73 | .85 | 1.41 | .64 | .67 |
| | C | 7 | 5 | 1 | 14 | 12-13 |
| Denmark | A | 21 | 25 | 83 | 151 | 97 |
| | B | .19 | .20 | .67 | 1.08 | .62 |
| | C | 16 | 16 | 11 | 6 | 14 |
| Germany | A | 782 | 1141 | 1664 | 2028 | 1487 |
| | B | .65 | .94 | 1.24 | 1.32 | .80 |
| | C | 8 | 4 | 3 | 2 | 8 |
| Norway | A | 17 | 30 | 59 | 75 | 67 |
| | B | .22 | .36 | .65 | .77 | .59 |
| | C | 15 | 15 | 12-13-14 | 9 | 16 |
| France | A | 1320 | 1341 | 1720 | 1710 | 1808 |
| | B | 1.22 | 1.15 | 1.35 | 1.22 | 1.24 |
| | C | 1-2 | 2 | 2 | 4 | 2 |
| Australia | A | 151 | 194 | 206 | 232 | 385 |
| | B | .63 | .74 | .73 | .74 | 1.12 |
| | C | 10 | 7 | 8-9-10 | 12 | 4 |
| Belgium | A | 178 | 164 | 243 | 257 | 309 |
| | B | .97 | .84 | 1.17 | 1.12 | 1.23 |
| | C | 4.5 | 6 | 4 | 5 | 3 |
| Netherlands | A | 254 | 228 | 275 | 369 | 457 |
| | B | 1.22 | .99 | 1.09 | 1.31 | 1.46 |
| | C | 1-2 | 3 | 5 | 3 | 1 |
| United Kingdom | A | 911 | 803 | 760 | 1146 | 1259 |
| | B | .85 | .73 | .74 | 1.04 | 1.04 |
| | C | 6 | 8 | 7 | 7 | 5 |

(*Contd.*)

(*Contd.*)

| | | 1966 | 1967 | 1968 | 1969 | 1970 (Prelim.) |
|---|---|---|---|---|---|---|
| Australia | A | 49 | 48 | 74 | 81 | 96 |
| | B | .49 | .44 | .65 | .65 | .67 |
| | C | 12 | 13 | 12-13-14 | 13 | 12-13 |
| Japan | A | 625 | 798 | 1030 | 1263 | 1824 |
| | B | .62 | .67 | .73 | .76 | .93 |
| | C | 11 | 10 | 8-9-10 | 10 | 7 |
| Italy | A | 632 | 287 | 550 | 848 | 725 |
| | B | .99 | .41 | .73 | 1.03 | .78 |
| | C | 3 | 14 | 8-9-10 | 8 | 9 |
| Portugal | A | 40 | 78 | 48 | 98 | 65 |
| | B | .97 | 1.71 | .96 | 1.75 | 1.02 |
| | C | 4-5 | 1 | 6 | 1 | 6 |

A = Total Net Flows (US$ millions)
B = Flow as percentage of GNP dollars
C = Rank of Members Based on Flow as percentage of GNP

*Source:* Canadian International Development Agency, Annual Review, Ottawa, Canada, 1971-72, p. 80.

What Gunnar Myrdal pointed out earlier is clearly visible in Tables 2.12 and 2.13. An analysis of the two tables clearly represents the same thing. In Table 2.12, the first column shows the yearly private investment of American companies, the figures in the second column do, however, completely offset the inflow of capital. The difference between the two columns, the profits transferred, and the inflow of investment capital, represents the net losses sustained by the developing nations as a result of the method used by the private US companies.

Now let us have a look at Table 2.13. It shows the investment of the American companies in the developed nations. The developed nations suffer no loss of foreign exchange with this investment. On the contrary, the developed nations receive even more than they pay out. This enormous profit in the former case (Table 2.12) is largely due to lower wages and cheap manpower and natural resources of the underdeveloped nations. Unfortunately, the developing nations have no other alternative at present but to suffer this tremendous amount of foreign exchange loss. But, in the long run, these things lead to bitterness and frustration and seriously endanger international peace and security. In spite of this, what is amazing is that this amount of money (Table 2.12, Column 1) is termed and accounted as 'aid'. In 1969, the total development aid[12] was $13.3 billion US dollars, of which only $4.4 billion US dollars, or about 33 per cent, was in the form of grants, the rest being commercial investment, which brings home even more money and is usually termed as 'aid'. If we analyze these figures, (Fig. 2.2), private investment has been increasing from 27.1 per cent in 1960-62 to, on the annual average, 32.4 per cent in 1969 (Table 2.12). As a whole, taking 1950 as a base figure, these non-equivalent trade and monopoly prices, it was found that in 1962 that the changed terms of trade meant a net loss[13] to the developing countries in excess of $3000 million US dollars. Such estimates were submitted to the 1964 UNCTAD held in Geneva. The reason why these profits from developing nations are repatriated to the capital exporting nations is that not much business is available in the poor nations to reinvest these huge profits, which is the difference between the two columns of Table 2.12. To compensate the deficit balance of payments and acute shortage of foreign exchange, as a result of this repatriation, official loans bearing a good interest are negotiated. These interests, amortization, and service payments help the developing nations to weaken[14] themselves even more. At the same time, the higher rate of population growth accelerates this weakening process. Thus, this situation clearly indicates that the underdeveloped nations and the decision variables in their development system are unrealistic. With the present system going on, the dimensions of misery and poverty and the problems of food, shelter, clothing and literacy can never be solved.

Now let us have a look at trade between developed and the underdeveloped nations. It looks like "rich men's club".

**Table 2.12:** Direct Investments and Profits of the United States Companies in the Liberated Countries

*(US$ millions)*

| *Year* | *Direct Capital Investment* | *Profits Transferred to USA* |
|---|---|---|
| 1959 | 525 | 1410 |
| 1960 | 229 | 1469 |
| 1961 | 419 | 1616 |
| 1962 | 203 | 1882 |
| 1963 | 451 | 1969 |
| 1964 | 523 | 2289 |
| 1965 | 807 | 2252 |
| 1966 | 519 | 2344 |

*Source:* L. Stepnov, "The problem of economic independence" in Y. Zhukov, *et al.*, (eds.), *The Third World*...(Moscow: Progress Pub., 1970); p. 114.

**Table 2.13:** Export of US Private Capital to Advanced Capitalist States and Repatriation of Profits—Yearly Average

*(US$ millions)*

| *Year* | *Direct Capital Investment* | *Profits Transferred to U.S.A.* |
|---|---|---|
| 1953-57 | 663 | 558 |
| 1958-62 | 1120 | 920 |

*Source:* L. Stepnov, "The problem of economic independence" in Y. Zhukov, *et al.*, (eds.), *The Third World*...(Moscow: Progress Pub., 1970); p. 114.

Tables 2.14, 2.15 and 2.16, present trade and its amount between the rich and the poor nations. Table 2.15 shows that trade in the period between 1953 and 1969 between rich and rich rose from $ 29 billion to $ 138 billion, while trade between rich and poor nations in the same period rose only from $ 14 billion to $ 36 billion or, in the other words, trade between rich and rich has grown to 475.8 per cent, while the trade between rich and poor grew 257 per cent and from poor to rich to only 233 per cent. We now need to centralize our efforts to trade between the two groups. The rich nations should not form a 'rich men's club'. This has been recommended in the Pearson Report[15]:

**Table 2.14:** Trade between Rich and Poor Countries

| | *Rich to Rich* | *Rich to Poor* |
|---|---|---|
| 1953 | US$ 29 billion | US$ 14 billion |
| 1969 | US$ 138 billion | US$ 36 billion |
| | *Poor to Rich* | *Poor to Rich* |
| 1953 | US$ 15 billion | US$ 5 billion |
| 1969 | US$ 35 billion | US$ 10 billion |

*Source:* Dudley Seers, "Rich Countries and Poor," in D. Seers and Joy, (eds.), *Development in a Divided World*, (Middlesex, England: Penguin, 1971); p. 20.

**Table 2.15:** International Transaction of all Poor Countries in 1963 (Actual) and 1975 (Projected)

*(Billions of US Dollars)*

| | *1963* | *1963 Low* | *1975 High* |
|---|---|---|---|
| 1. Exports of goods and services at 1960 prices | 87.6 | 67.5 | 73.5 |
| 2. Imports of goods and services at 1960 prices | 87.6 | 70.9 | 83.5 |
| 3. Factor income interest & profit | 4.9 | 12.0 | 14.2 |
| 4. Technical assistance | 1.0 | 1.5 | 1.5 |
| 5. Trade gap | 1 – (2+3+4) | 16.9 | 25.7 |
| 6. Official aid net | 6.6 | 8.5 | 12.9 |
| 7. Private capital net | 8.8 | 4.4 | 5.4 |
| 8. Unfilled | 5 – (6+7) | 4.0 | 7.4 |

* The low and high corresponds to rates of growth, low 5.2 per cent for poor countries and 4.2 per cent for rich countries High 6.1 per cent for poor countries and 4.7 per cent for rich countries.

** Expenditures, salaries of exports and consultants usually financed by aid.

*Source:* UNCTAD, 2nd Session 1967, Documents TD/34/Suppl and TD/34 Supp. 1/Add. 1.

Oscar Braun "External Economic Strategy; Outward or Inward looking" in D. Seers and Joy, (eds.), *Development in a Divided World*, (Middle Sex, England; Penguin, 1971); p. 155.

**Table 2.16:** Exports of Manufactured goods from developing areas**

*(US$ billions)*

| | *1953* | *1959* | *1965* |
|---|---|---|---|
| Exports of Manufactures | | | |
| (a) To developed countries | 0.80 | 1.48 | 2.80 |
| (b) To other developing countries | 0.65 | 0.65 | 1.35 |
| Total | 1.50 | 2.10 | 4.25 |
| Of which from | | | |
| Hong Kong | 0.19 | 0.37 | 0.84 |
| India | 0.54 | 0.55 | 0.79 |
| Israel | 0.04 | 0.11 | 0.30 |
| Taiwan | 0.01 | 0.04 | 0.23 |

*Source:* UNCTAD, 2nd Session 1967, Documents TD/34/Suppl. and TD/34 Supp. 1/Add. 1.

Oscar Braun "External Economic Strategy; Outward or Inward Looking" in D. Seers and Joy, (eds.), *Development in a Divided World*, (Middle Sex, England; Penguin, 1971); p. 166.

> *"We recommend that bilateral donors and international agencies provide financial assistance to institutions such as development banks and clearing and payment unions which are designed to promote trade among the developing countries on a regional scale."*

It further says that[16]:

> *"We recommend that regional development banks, in cooperation with other international agencies, take the lead in making available special funds for the re-financing of export credits granted by developing countries, and in establishing regional export credit insurance facilities."*

For the benefits of the underdeveloped nations, increased trade is more important than granting aids and loans, etc. The burden of loans requires heavy repayment of interests, which in turn creates the serious problem of deficit in balance of payments. The scarcity of foreign exchange then becomes even more acute.

Any development project carried out in any underdeveloped area, financed by developed nations on a bilateral basis, especially during initial stages of take off, usually becomes bottlenecked if the recipient nation does not meet the selfish ends of the donor nation. Under the influence of the intensified cold war, and after the Korean war in particular, development programmes for underdeveloped countries were actually shaped so as to be in the political and economic interests of the developed nations and particularly those of the United States. The political, military and strategic motives have continuously been given primary attention. In 1965, Ian Smith unilaterally declared Rhodesia's independence and the Harold Wilson's Labour government took no meaningful steps to protect the 92 per cent of Rhodesia's[17] population who were then at the mercy of the racist regime. In accordance with a resolution of the Organization of African Unity, President Nyerere of Tanzania protested by breaking off diplomatic relations with Britain. Britain retaliated by freezing $ 7,500,000 worth of aid to Tanzania. If proof was needed of the political nature of the aid, it was this. During the India-Pakistan war in 1965, the Government of US even suspended the food aid to India. The war in Vietnam certainly was a burning example of the US Government and her military policies, sacrificing even the UN Charter, Universal Declaration of Human Rights, all humanitarian grounds, and world opinion. Myrdal[18] said, "When politics goes into aid, whether at home or abroad, it is unavoidable that standards both of morality and of effectiveness are apt to be radically lowered". The development of the underdeveloped can never be achieved if politics and aid are tied together.

Now let us have a look at Table 2.17. This Table shows annual bilateral and multilateral assistance to major recipient countries. As pointed out earlier, only about 10 per cent of the total aid goes through multilateral assistance, the rest being on a bilateral basis. I would like to mention distinctions between the natures of aid for reasons of:

1. Meeting political selfish ends, and
2. On humanitarian grounds to help the underdeveloped.

**Table 2.17:** Selected Measures of Annual Bilateral and Multilateral Assistance to Major Recipients: 1964-67 Average

| *Main Recipient* | *Total Net Official Flow* | | *Population* | *Total Net Official Flow* | | |
|---|---|---|---|---|---|---|
| | *$ Millions* | *% of Total* | *Millions* | *$ per Capita* | *As % of GDP* | *As % of Imports* |
| Total All Less-Developed Countries | 6.754 | 100.0 | 1632.4 | 4.1 | 2.2 | – |
| India | 1.226 | 18.2 | 501.7 | 2.4 | 3.2 | 42.9 |
| Pakistan | 496 | 7.3 | 118.6 | 4.2 | 3.7 | 49.1 |

*Source:* Laster B. Pearson, Partners in Development (New York: Praeger Pub. 1969), p. 392.

The total net official, per capita, ranges from $ 1.0 (only one dollar) to $ 177.1. In countries like Indonesia, Mexico, Nigeria, Philippines, Brazil, India, etc., it ranges from per capita (between 1964 and 1967) annual average $ 1.0 to $ 2.4 (only two dollars and forty cents). Here it would be pertinent to mention that population in India alone totals more than that of the continents of Africa and Latin America. The aids to countries like French DOM TOM Africa and French DOM TOM America is $ 115.7 and $ 177.1, respectively, per capita. Again, countries like Israel, Papua, and New Guinea, Jordan, Laos, South Vietnam, etc. receive, per capita, (on the annual average between 1964-67) $ 44.2, $ 38.2, $ 31.9, $ 23.7, and $ 23.0 per capita. Now all these countries that receive this aid, excluding the French overseas departments and territories in south and central America and Africa, receive much higher aid from 1 to 44.20 per capita. The former (per capita) is Indonesia and the latter (44.2 per capita) is Israel. Thus, the percentage of development aid might range from 1 per capita to 44.2 per capita, depending upon political leverage. With this scenario I doubt if the underdeveloped people would ever be able to develop, as far as development from foreign assistance is concerned.

Aid should be based on moral and humanitarian grounds. It is an international issue, not just something within the political and economic outlook of the interests of the donor nations. The political nature of aid, as a matter of fact, does not take into consideration the real economic needs of the recipient country but rather the fact that they are 'gifts'. The donor nations should not have aid involved in any military or political commitment.

Another aspect of aid that I would like to point out in the typing of aid and loans to exports only from the donor nations. This sometimes becomes undue exploitation. This condition does not allow the recipient nation to invite international tenders, and thus cannot export or buy at a competitive market price. The recipient nation is denied higher prices, because it is denied the opportunity to scan the international market. This typing of aid to export gives the donor nation a surplus in her balance of payments. In this type of bilateral exchange, when the interests of the recipient nation conflicts with those of the donor nation, the interests of the recipient nation are mercilessly sacrificed.

The attitude of all the donor nations is not alike. The governments of Sweden, Canada, and Netherlands have usually been providing aids, loans and grants to the underdeveloped to help them fight the problems of lack of food, shelter, clothing and literacy without political motivations and without unduly typing their assistance to exports. The governments of Switzerland, Norway, Finland, and Denmark were equally praiseworthy. The governments of Britain, France, West Germany and Japan pursued a more militant course in the 1960s in tying up their aid with this or that[19] I would like to conclude this topic with the following observations which must be implemented:

1. We recommend that provisions in aid agreements which limit the rights of recipients to invite competitive tenders should be suspended immediately.
2. DAC members meeting, held in Tokyo in September 1970, declared their willingness to an agreement for the untying of their bilateral financial loans.

If the present trend continues and the above recommendations are not implemented, I am sure that underdeveloped nations are now determined to achieve their economic independence in the way they achieved their political independence, struggling hard for centuries, bearing hardships, and tolerating frustrations.

## B. FOREIGN DEBT AND AID: THE SITUATION DURING 1980-1990

In the preceding Section A of this chapter, an in-depth analysis of the role of foreign debt and aid in the task of nation building was carried out from 1950 to 1970.

We now attempt to provide data on aid, debt, interests, and amortization for the 1980-90 period.

Summed-up data for India from 1980 to 2001 are given in Table 2.18 (A to G) which include (A) Foreign debt, (B) Interest paid, (C) Principal amount paid, (D) DSR, (E) Exchange rate of rupee, (F) Net outflow from India and (G) Import-Export balance.

This Table 2.18 (A to G) shows that an amount of Rs. 4,81,224 crore (approx. $ 100 billion) is outstanding as foreign debt in 2001 despite Rs. 72,558 crore paid as principal amount and Rs. 46,923 crore paid as interest during the decade of so called reforms that began in their enhanced form in 1991. New loans are now being negotiated just to pay principal and interest on earlier loans so as to keep those "old" loans as "current".

The foreign debt of India is constantly on the rise from 1980 onwards till 2002 despite so much amount of principal and interest is constantly being paid every year since then. Since mid-1999, despite all the assistance and all the loans from foreign countries, the net amount is being flown from out of India to the foreign lenders as shown in Table 2.18(F), which is nearly Rs. 1,000 crore in 2000, and Rs. 3,000 crore in 2001.

The value of Dollar has risen six times against the Rupee during the twenty-year period from 1980 to 2001, i.e. from Rs. 7 in 1981 to Rs. 48 in 2001; and nearly three times during the ten-year of reforms, i.e. from Rs. 17 in 1991 to Rs. 48 in 2001. The exports of India have also been falling short of imports during every year of these ten years of reforms from 1991 to 2001. During these ten years, imports at Rs. 13,55,000 crore and exports at Rs. 11,39,000 crore, give a net shortage of exports at Rs. 2,16,000 (-ve).

## Table 2.18: (A to G)

(A) Foreign debt, (B) Interest paid, (C) Principal amount paid, (D) Debt Service Ratio (DSR), (E) Exchange rate of rupee, (F) Net outflow from India and (G) Import-Export balance for India from 1980 to 2001.

**Table 2.18(A):** Foreign debt of India from 1980 to 2001

| *Year* | *US$ million* | *Current Value in Rs. 48/$ (in Rs. crores)* |
|---|---|---|
| 1980 | 20,610 | 98,928 |
| 1985 | 36,625 | 1,75,800 |
| 1990 | 70,115 | 3,36,552 |
| 2000 | 99,088 | 4,75,622 |
| 2001 | 1,00,255 | 4,81,224 |

*Source:* Statistical Outline of India, 2001-2002, Tata Services Limited, Mumbai, December 2001 and earlier editions.

**Table 2.18(B):** Interest paid by India on Foreign Debt from 1980 to 2001

| *Year* | *Interest paid in Rs. crores* | |
|---|---|---|
| 1980-81 | 286 | |
| 1990-91 | 1,954 | |
| Total 1980-91 | | 9,333 |
| 1991-92 | 3,006 | |
| 1992-93 | 3,961 | |
| 1993-94 | 4,199 | |
| 1994-95 | 4,635 | |
| 1995-96 | 5,083 | |
| 1996-97 | 4,870 | |
| 1997-98 | 4,795 | |
| 1998-99 | 5,192 | |
| 1999-2000 | 5,480 | |
| 2000-01 | 5,702 | |
| Total 1991-2001 | | 46,923 |
| Total 1980-2001 | | 56,256 |

*Source:* Statistical Outline of India, 2001-2002, Tata Services Limited, Mumbai, December 2001 and earlier editions.

**Table 2.18(C):** Principal paid by India on Foreign Debt from 1980 to 2001

| *Year* | *Principal paid in Rs. crores* | |
|---|---|---|
| 1980-81 | 518 | |
| 1990-91 | 2,329 | |
| Total 1980-91 | | 2,847 |
| 1991-92 | 3,650 | |
| 1992-93 | 4,788 | |
| 1993-94 | 5,353 | |
| 1994-95 | 5,791 | |
| 1995-96 | 7,566 | |
| 1996-97 | 7,070 | |
| 1997-98 | 7,550 | |
| 1998-99 | 8,880 | |
| 1999-2000 | 9,686 | |
| 2000-01 | 12,254 | |
| Total 1991-2001 | | 72,588 |
| Total 1980-2001 | | 75,435 |

*Source:* Statistical Outline of India, 2001-2002, Tata Services Limited, Mumbai, December 2001 and earlier editions.

**Table 2.18(D):** Debt Service Ratio (DSR) of India from 1980-2001

| *Year* | *DSR* |
|---|---|
| *1980* | 7.6 |
| *1990* | 32.7 |
| *1999* | 15 |

*Source:* Statistical Outline of India, 2001-2002, Tata Services Limited, Mumbai, December 2001 and earlier editions. The DSR (Debt Service Ratio) is defined as p. 280.

**Table 2.18(E):** Exchange rate of Indian rupee versus $ from 1980 to 2001

| *Year* | *Rs. for 1 $* |
|---|---|
| 1981 | 7.91 |
| 1986 | 12.24 |
| 1991 | 17.94 |
| 1996 | 34.35 |
| 2001 | (approx.) 48.00 |

*Source:* Statistical Outline of India, 2001-2002, Tata Services Limited, Mumbai, December 2001 and earlier editions.

**Table 2.18(F):** Total Debt Received, Amounts of Amortization and Interest Paid, and Net Inflow during the Decade 1991-2001

| *Year* | *Assistance* | | *Amortization* | | *Interest* | | *Net Inflow* | |
|---|---|---|---|---|---|---|---|---|
| | $ million | Rs. crores at current prices 2002 | $ million | Rs. crores at current prices 2002 | $ million | Rs. crores at current prices 2002 | $ million | Rs. crores at current prices 2002 |
| 1991-92 | 4746 | 22,780 | 1491 | 7,156 | 1228 | 5,894 | 2026 | 9,724 |
| 1992-93 | 3583 | 17,198 | 1562 | 7,497 | 1292 | 6,201 | 729 | 3,499 |
| 1993-94 | 3756 | 18,028 | 1707 | 8,193 | 1339 | 6,427 | 711 | 3,412 |
| 1994-95 | 3484 | 16,723 | 1844 | 8,851 | 1476 | 7,084 | 164 | 787 |
| 1995-96 | 3295 | 15,816 | 2262 | 10,857 | 1520 | 7,296 | -486 | -2,332 |
| 1996-97 | 3374 | 16,195 | 1992 | 9,561 | 1372 | 6,585 | 11 | 52 |
| 1997-98 | 3177 | 15,249 | 2031 | 9,748 | 1290 | 6,192 | -145 | -696 |
| 1998-99 | 3147 | 15,105 | 2111 | 10,132 | 1234 | 5,923 | -198 | -950 |
| 1999-00 | 3299 | 15,835 | 2235 | 10,728 | 1265 | 6,072 | -201 | -964 |
| 2000-01 | 3120 | 14,976 | 2553 | 12,254 | 1188 | 5,702 | -621 | -2,980 |

*Source:* S.S. Anklesaria Aiyar, Who needs foreign aid from the World Bank and IMF anyway?, *Times of India,* New Delhi, March 31, 2002, p. 15 (Reserve Bank of India). Indian Rs. is calculated for approximation at Rs. 48 per US $ at the current exchange rate.

**Table 2.18(G):** Import-Export of India with Balance from 1990-2001

| *Year* | *Rs. 000 crores* | | |
|---|---|---|---|
| | *Import* | *Export* | *Balance* |
| 1990-91 | 32.5 | 43.1 | –10.6 |
| 1991-92 | 44.0 | 47.8 | –3.8 |
| 1992-93 | 53.6 | 63.3 | –9.6 |
| 1993-94 | 69.7 | 73.1 | –3.3 |
| 1994-95 | 82.6 | 89.9 | –7.2 |
| 1995-96 | 1,06.3 | 1,22.6 | –16.3 |
| 1996-97 | 1,18.8 | 1,38.9 | –20.1 |
| 1997-98 | 1,30.1 | 1,54.1 | –24.0 |
| 1998-99 | 1,39.7 | 1,78.3 | –38.5 |
| 1999-2000 | 1,59.5 | 2,15.5 | –55.9 |
| 2000-01 | 2,01.6 | 2,27.5 | –25.8 |
| Total | 11,38.8 | 13,55.0 | –2,16.0 |

*Source:* Annual Reference Book: India 2002, Publications Division, Ministry of Information and Broadcasting, Govt. of India, New Delhi, pp. 605-06.

The Debt Service Ratio (DSR) has certainly improved during this decade of reforms from 32.7 in 1991 to 15 in 2001 but at what cost to the people of India! The value of Rupee has nearly fallen three times during this decade of reforms from Rs. 17 in 1980 to Rs. 48 in 2001 and exorbitant amount of interest on foreign debt is being paid from securing the new loans! Is this a sign of a developing economy? Certainly not.

The data are now given for developing countries as a whole, and between several groups of developing countries such as low income, middle income, low-and-middle income economies. The data are also given for each country in South Asia and China. Total private debt, total external debt and debt-service ratios as a percentage of GNP and exports of goods and services are given.

Table 2.19 provides data on total external debt for 1990 and 1998 for all countries in South Asia, China and all developing countries.

Table 2.20 provides data on DSR for 1990 and 1999 as per cent of export of goods and services for all countries in South Asia, China and all developing countries.

**Table 2.19.** Total External Debt for 1990 and 1998 for all Countries in South Asia, China and all Developing Countries

| *Country/Region* | *Debt in US$ millions* | |
|---|---|---|
| | *1990* | *1998* |
| Bangladesh | 12,769 | 16,376 |
| India | 83,717 | 98,232 |
| Myanmar | 4,695 | 5,680 |
| Nepal | 1,640 | 2,646 |
| Pakistan | 20,663 | 32,229 |
| Sri Lanka | 5,863 | 8,526 |
| China | 55,301 | 154,599 |
| Low Income | 418,922 | 579,545 |
| Middle Income | 1,041,421 | 1,956,501 |
| Low and Middle Income (or developing countries as a whole) | 1,460,343 | 2,536,046 |
| South Asia | 129,899 | 163,775 |

*Source:* The World Bank, *The World Development Report 2000/2001*, Oxford University Press, New York, 2000, pp. 314-15.

**Table 2.20:** DSR as per cent of Export of Goods and Services for 1990 and 1999 for all Countries in South Asia, China and all Developing Countries

| *HDI Rank* | *Country/Region* | *Total Debt Service as % of exports of goods and services* | |
|---|---|---|---|
| | | *1990* | *1999* |
| 81 | Sri Lanka | 13.7 | 7.9 |
| 115 | India | 32.7 | 15.0 |
| 127 | Pakistan | 23.0 | 30.5 |
| 129 | Nepal | 13.4 | 7.9 |
| 130 | Bhutan | 5.5 | 4.8 |
| 132 | Bangladesh | 28.4 | 10.1 |
| 87 | China | 11.7 | 9.0 |
| | Developing Countries | 18.7 | 22.3 |
| | Least Developed Countries | 15.5 | 13.0 |
| | South Asia | 20.0 | 16.6 |
| | High Income | – | – |
| | Middle Income | 16.9 | 21.8 |
| | Low Income | 26.6 | 18.8 |

*Source:* United Nations Development Programme, *Human Development Report 2001*, Oxford University Press, New York, 2001, pp. 192-94.

The growth of external debt for developing countries as a whole from 1982 to 1991 is given in Table 2.21. From this Table, it can be seen that the debt of the developing countries has constantly been on the rise.

**Table 2.21:** Growth of External Debt of Developing Countries from 1982 to 1991, year-wise

| *Year* | *$ billions* |
|---|---|
| 1982 | 831 |
| 1983 | 894 |
| 1984 | 933 |
| 1985 | 1,051 |
| 1986 | 1,152 |
| 1987 | 1,281 |
| 1988 | 1,320 |
| 1989 | 1,300 |
| 1990 | 1,350 |
| 1991 | 1,350 |

*Sources:* World Debt Tables, Vol.I, 1988-89 Edition, The World Bank Washington DC, 1988; p. X.

*The Economic Times*, New Delhi, 17-12-1991; Editorial, p. 10.

## Low, Medium and High Income Economies

The World Bank classifies economies for operational and analytical purposes primarily by GNP per capita. Every economy is classified as low income, middle income (subdivided into lower middle and upper middle), or high income. ...Low-income and middle-income economies are sometines referred to as developing economies. ...The groups are as follows: low income, $755 or less; lower middle income, $756-2,995; upper middle income, $2,996-9,265; and high income, $9,266 or more (The World Bank, *World Development Report, 2000/2001*, Oxford University Press, New York, 2000, p. 335).

## Human Development Index (HDI)

The HDI measures the overall achievements in a country in three basic dimensions of human development longevity, knowledge and a decent standard of living. It is measured by life expectancy, educational attainment (adult literacy and combined primary, secondary and tertiary enrolment) and adjusted income per capita in purchasing power parity (PPP) US dollars. The HDI is a summary, not a comprehensive measure of human development (*Human Development Report 2001*, UNDP, Oxford University Press, New York, 2001, p. 14).

## Human Poverty Index (HPI)

While the HDI measures overall progress in a country in achieving human development, the human poverty index (HPI) reflects the distribution of progress and measures the backlog of deprivations that still exists. The HPI measures deprivation in the same dimensions of basic human development as the HDI (*Human Development Report 2001*, UNDP, Oxford University Press, New York, 2001, p. 14).

The debt service ratio, as a percentage of export of goods and services varies from country to country, but it is around

30 per cent or more for most of the countries including India, causing the so called "debt-trap" in the contemporary international monitory phraseology.

Let us now look at the official development "aid" from rich countries to the poor countries.

Table 2.22 gives data on official developmental assistance separately from each of the OECD and the OPEC countries, i.e. the total development assistance provided by rich countries to the poor countries.

**Table 2.22:** Official Development Assistance from 1970 to 1989

*(US$ millions)*

| *Year* | *From OECD* | *From OPEC* |
|---|---|---|
| 1970 | 6968 | – |
| 1975 | 13855 | – |
| 1980 | 27296 | 9636 |
| 1985 | 29429 | 3615 |
| 1986 | 36663 | 4704 |
| 1987 | 41595 | 3328 |
| 1988 | 48114 | 2409 |
| 1989 | 46697 | – |

*Source*: Data condensed from *World Development Report, 1991*, The World Bank, Washington DC, 1991; p. 240.

The official development assistance from major OECD countries in 1989 stood at US$ 46697 million, i.e. .038 per cent of the total of US$ 1300 x 1000 million. This official assistance is thus less than half per cent of the total debt. This official assistance is less than one per cent of the GNP of the most of the donor countries, with that of the US being only 0.25 per cent of GNP, the single largest donor.

The debt service ratio, as a percentage of export of goods and services varies from country to country, but it is around 30 per cent or more for most of the countries including India, causing the so called "debt-trap" in the contemporary international monitory phraseology.

The DSR (Debt Service Ratio) of the various regions of the World are given in Tables 2.23(a) and 2.23(b) which is close to 19 per cent for South Asia. This DSR has come down from over 30 per cent in the early 1990s to 20 per cent in late 1990s. The total debt of India at the end of 2001 stud and approximately $100 billion or Rs. 4,67,589 crore.

The value of Indian Rupee for 1 $ in 1980 was less than Rs. 8, touching to Rs. 18 ten years later in 1990-91 and jumping to Rs. 48 further after ten years later in 2000-01. Hence Indian Rupee has been sliding down like anything, which is skyrocketing the amount of debt.

**Table 2.23(a):** Total Debt Service Ratios as per cent of receipts of India, 1980-1993

| | *Year* | *Ratio* |
|---|---|---|
| 1. | 1980 | 7.9 |
| | 1985 | 17.5 |
| | 1986 | 21.2 |
| | 1987 | 21.6 |
| 2. | 1988 | 29.8 |
| | 1989 | 26.5 |
| 3. | 1990 | 30.9 |
| | 1992 | 30.7 |
| | 1993 | 30.4 |

*Sources*:

1. *Statistical Outline of India*, 1989-90, Tata Services Ltd., Bombay 1989, p. 152;
2. *Statistical Outline of India*, 1992-93, Tata Services Ltd., Bombay, 1992, p. 148;
3. *The Hindustan Times*, New Delhi, 5-11-1993, p. 19.

**Table 2.23(b):** Debt Service Ratio of the Various Regions of The World

| *Region* | *Debt Service Ratio (1998)* |
|---|---|
| | Hdr-p222 |
| All developing countries | 20.1 |
| Least developed countries | 13.1 |
| East Asia | 10.5 |
| East Asia (Excluding China) | 12.9 |
| Latin America & Carabbean | 33.7 |
| South Asia | 18.9 |
| South Asia (Excluding India) | 16.7 |
| SE Asia & Pacific | 17.3 |
| Sub-Saharan Africa | 15.1 |
| Eastern Europe and the CIS | 13.5 |
| Middle Income | 20.2 |
| Low Income | 15.1 |
| World | 18.9 |

*Source:* UNDP, *Human Development Report 2000*, Oxford University Press, New York, 2000, p. 222.

So the amount of interest on debt would also continue to drain the economy. This then becomes a vicious circle so which country can develop with debt from Western powers, IMF, World Bank, etc. The amount of debt has also been rising for the last 20 years despite substantial amounts being paid as amortization and interest. New loans are being negotiated to pay for amortization and interest on earlier loans for the last 20 years. This is debt-trap.

## C. THE DEBT-TRAP

**Who aids whom?**

**The poor nations to rich nations!**

> *"Many countries in Asia and Africa have not yet reached the standards that South Korea had reached in the mid-1950s. Progress, particularly since the 1980s, has been hampered by the withdrawal of money from human development expenditure to cover debt repayment. ...As an additional disconcerting variable, moderate to severe debt has touched virtually all developing countries. The unprecedented flow of resources from the developing countries into the core around the turn of the century into as even more painful, slower, lopsided and chaotic process it otherwise already would have been."*
>
> *Kristoffel Lieten*[20]*, 2001*

In the preceding two Sections A and B of this chapter, the data covering debt and aid from developed countries to the developing countries were provided from 1950 to 1970 and from 1970 to 1990s, respectively.

An attempt is now made to analyze the "role" and impact of this debt and aid syndrome in the development and modernization of poor countries.

In 1980, an Independent Commission on International Development Issues, under the Chairmanship of Nobel Prize winner for Peace and former Chancellor of then West Germany, Willy Brandt[21], published a Report in 1980, entitled: North-

South: A Programme for Survival. The members of the Commission were internationally renowned experts in their respective fields. Some of the recommendations concerning with debt and aid made out in this report were meant to be implemented during the 1980-85 period. They are given below[22]:

> "The flow of official development finance should be enlarged by:
>
> 1. An international system of universal revenue mobilization, based on a sliding scale related to national income, in which East European and developing countries—except the poorest countries—would participate.
> 2. The adoption of timetables to increase Official Development Assistance from industrialized countries to the level of 0.7 per cent of GNP by 1985, and to one per cent before the end of the century.
> 3. Introduction of automatic revenue transfers through international levies on some of the following: international trade, arms production or exports; international travel; the global commons, especially seabed minerals.
>
> Lending through international financial institutions should be improved through:
>
> 1. Effective utilization of the increased borrowing capacity of the World Bank, resulting from the recent decision to double its capital to $80 billion.
> 2. Doubling the borrowing-to-capital ratio of the World Bank from its present gearing of 1:1 to 2:1, and similar action by Regional Development Banks.
> 3. Abstaining from the imposition of political conditions on the operations of multilateral financial institutions.
> 4. Channeling an increasing share of development finance through regional institutions.
> 5. A substantial increase in programme lending.

6. The use of IMF gold reserves either for further sales, whole profits would subsidize interest on development lending, or as collateral to borrow for on-lending to developing countries.
7. Giving borrowing countries a greater role in decision-making and management."

None of the above recommendations of the Commission under the chairmanship of Willy Brandt has been implemented, though they were meant to be implemented by the rich nations from 1980 to 1985. For this reason, the economic situation of the poor countries has begun to slide to a pathetic situation.

It is rather part of a sad commentary in international arena that literally none of the recommendations made out in that Report has really been implemented. What has been implemented is something different altogether. Several attempts have been made, particularly since 1985, what a report of the World Bank published in December 1988, it called, *"to refinance a proportion of interest due, so as to keep loans current."*[23] This Report further concluded that, "though some achievements have been made, an end to the debt-crisis remains elusive...most of the indebted countries are still (in 1988-89) no better off than in 1982—when the debt-crisis erupted." Commenting on this issue of the unbearable burden of foreign debt and interest on the shattered economies of the poor countries, the President of the World Bank, Barber B. Conable[24], said in London on April 27, 1989, at a meeting organized by Reuters:

> "...Everyone must do his share. The debtor country must have the courage and determination to implement an appropriate policy matrix. The bilateral lenders must supplement the resources of the multilateral agencies, and must improve the regulatory and tax environment to facilitate commercial bank cooperation. The commercial banks must be willing to provide debt or debt service reduction consistent with market realities and/or new money as appropriate. And the multilateral agencies must provide policy advice, technical assistance, adjustment

loans, financing to help reduce debt, coordination of available resources and instrument-design tailored to country circumstance."

All of these suggestions from the World Bank in 1989 amount literally to nothing than what the Independent Commission on Internal Developmental issues under the chairmanship of Willy Brandt[25] had noted in 1980:

> "As the loans fall due, they need to borrow more in order to repay and service them. ...The debt servicing record of developing countries has been excellent on the whole and payments crises have been rare. But there are likely to be more difficulties with payments in the future."

What it amounts to is fairly clear. All attempt to "resolve" the debt-crisis since 1982, when the debt-crisis first erupted, centring on "re-structuring" of the poor countries' economies, a lowering of a percentage point or so on interest rates, sanctioning new loans to pay interest so the debt could remain "current", further devaluation of the poor countries' currencies, etc. are measures which simply cannot provide any relief from debt-crisis. Professor Valentin Shehetinin[26], a noted authority on international development economics, rightly says "that no genuine settlement of the foreign debt problem is possible without a restructuring of international economic relations on a just and equal basis." This just and equal base can only be the interest of the poor countries. Without this just and equal base, which the moneylenders of the rich countries continue to ignore for their selfish reasons to make money in the form of interests on their loans, contributes nothing to the economic development of the poor countries.

Mortgage the nation's economic control with the Western moneylenders! Why not? After all, the State in India is the "personal property", as Arun Shourie[27], a noted scholar and an eminent journalist, remarked. This statement of Shourie is much more true now 20 years later than when it was said in 1980 when India had negotiated a big loan at that time from the World Bank-IMF. There is apparently no need to mention the national humiliation that goes with this kind of borrowing. The agony of this whole scenario is pretty bizarre: the prospective nation first must carry a 'begging bowl', and if endowed with "charity" it must allow its economy's control and plunder by the moneylenders. Yet more bizarre is the fact that this exploitation is blatantly carried out under the philanthropic banner of "helping the helpless".

Obviously, commenting on such unjust and unequal bases, and the overall negative contribution of the foreign debt and aid, what Lester R. Pearson, former Prime Minister of Canada and a Nobel laureate for Peace, said is much more true in 1990 than when it was said over two decades ago in 1969. Pearson[28], said that:

> "On the whole, the evidence suggests that economic assistance has, at best, made little contribution to the aided nations' growth and, at worst, has seriously distorted it. ... Aid) too, perpetuates what is in essence a colonial relationship."

It is apparently this realization, which led the then President of Tanzania, Julius K. Nyerere[29], to say in 1967:

> "To burden the people with loans, the repayment of which will be beyond their means, is not to help them but to make them suffer."

What was said in 1967 is worse today in 1990s than it was in the late 1960s. Payment of interest and amortization on the debts has hampered all the socio-economic developmental efforts of the developing countries to the extent that, as emphasized again by Nyerere, in his capacity as Chairman of the South Commission, sanctioned by the Non-Aligned Movement as agreed to in 1986 in *Zimbabwe, in the Report,* entitled *The Challenge to the South: The Report of the South Commission*, Published in 1990[30]:

> "The time has come therefore for effective multilateral action to scale down the debt and reduce the burden of debt service to tolerable levels. In most cases, the debt crisis

> has turned out to be a crisis of solvency rather than merely of liquidity. ...The upshot is that debt has become a form of bondage, and the indebted economies have become indentured economies—a clear manifestation of neo-colonialism. This state of affairs cannot go on. The debt and its service must be reduced to a level that allows growth to proceed at an acceptable pace. ...We reaffirm the need for an International Debt Conference with the participation of the debtor governments, the governments of the creditors, and the international financial institutions, whose mandate would be to arrive at a binding international agreement on a framework solution."

It is rather sad to note that the problem of debt has been mentioned as a "bondage" in the Report of the South Commission, Published by Oxford in 1990, titled, *The Challenge to the South,* prepared under the Chairmanship of Nyerere sanctioned by NAM (Non-Aligned Movement) in 1986 in Zimbabwe.

On the surface, the intention behind borrowing and getting aid is to have some help in the task of economic development of the poor countries. But what is actually happening since 1984 is that there is a net transfer of funds from the poor countries to the rich nations. This is the real paradox. On a total debt of developing countries of $ 1350 billion in 1991[31], there has been a total debt service of $ 167.4 billion, interest payment of 74.1 billion, the net transfer on debt being $ 15.9 billion. Professor Altaf Gauher[32], while commenting on the lenders' fraud on the Third World, recommended that:

> "In aggregate terms the principal borrowed by the developing countries has been paid at least twice....The debtor countries have now become net exporters of capital to the creditor countries.
>
> The time has come for the developing countries to say enough is enough. They do not owe any money either in respect of the capital originally borrowed or in respect of interest charges calculated on a reasonable fixed rate basis.

> They should ask the creditors to count the profits they have made through this unconscionable exercise.
>
> Today's politics demands that the creditor countries and financial institutions must be made to stop this bleeding operation."

Furthermore, the 40 ministers of the least developed countries, who assembled at Cartage for the eighth session of the UNCTAD in February 1992, sought[33]:

> "Ministers of over 40 least developed countries (LDCs) have sought cancellation of all bilateral official debts and urgent measures for reduction of LDCs debt stocks and debt servicing burdens, including those due to multilateral financial institutions and commercial debts.
>
> The ministers in a communiqué adopted at their meeting here noted that the LDCs external debt burden continued to be a major hindrance to their development efforts..."

All talks on rescheduling of debt is nothing but borrowing more to pay-off interest to keep the old loans as current ones. This does not help the poor countries. Since the rich countries have already received almost twice of what was originally given as debt, they should now write-off all the existing loans or else there is no way out of this debt crisis. If this does not happen, the rich countries shall continue to exploit the precarious position of the poor countries, all obviously in the name of loans and aids to help the economic development of the poor countries. With this plunder of the poor countries by the rich countries, the poverty-stricken masses of the developing countries will simply continue to suffer, as they have been suffering for nearly the last 5 decades after the disintegration of the direct political colonialism in the aftermath of the Second World War since 1945.

Instead of helping the poor countries, the rich countries, through a subtle mechanism of debt and aid being implemented through the IMF and the World Bank combine, have began to control the economies of not only the smaller countries in the developing World but the giants of them such as Brazil, Mexico, Argentina in the 1980s and have now also got in their paws India as well in the beginning of 1990s.

The pathetic situation of these Latin American giants in the 1980s is bound to be repeated in India in the 1990s for the borrowing by India from the IMF and the World Bank since 1985 in general, and from 1991 in particular, are clearly based on the fact that India had to give the control and direction of the Indian economy in the hands of the IMF and the World Bank, as evident from the letter issued by the Finance Minister of India to the IMF dated November 11, 1991, reproduced below[34]:

"Dear Mr. Preston,

1. The Government of India has adopted a package of major policy reforms aimed at macro economic stabilization and restoration of the growth momentum to the economy. These initiatives are being implemented at a time when the Indian economy faces a serious balance of payments crisis. The strategy consists of measures aimed at achieving a sharp reduction in the fiscal deficit, combined with reforms in the key areas of trade policy, industrial policy, the public sector and the financial sector. The effectiveness of these measures in bringing about the desired structural adjustments in the economy while maintaining the momentum of growth depends critically upon the availability of adequate external finance. Accordingly, we are requesting a structural adjustment loan/credit from the World Bank. We believe that the policies outlined by us are adequate and sufficient to meet the objectives of the programme.
2. It is also our intention to seek IBRD/IDA support for our medium term reforms strategy through a series of structural/sectoral adjustment loans/credits, including fast disbursing support for establishing and

strengthening the social safety net to mitigate the social burden of the transition process.

3. We have no doubt that with continued support from multilateral financing institutions, particularly the Bank and the Fund, and given the resilience of our economy as well as the support of the international community as a whole, witnessed at a recent meeting of the Aid India Consortium, India would be able to overcome the present economic difficulties and return to a path of sustained high growth. I greatly look forward to your continued support in our endeavour to achieve these objectives.
4. The medium term reform program of the government is described in the attachment to this letter.

Kind regards,

Yours sincerely,
Sd/-
Manmohan Singh

*Mr. L.T. Preston,*
*President,*
*The World Bank,*
*Washington DC"*

The data regarding amount of foreign debt and interest paid by India were provided in the preceding Section B. The debt service ratio of India has increased from 9 per cent in 1980 to 30 per cent in 1991. From these figures, it is clear beyond doubt that India is rapidly heading towards the debt-trap in the 1990s. This debt-trap seems to have been well assured by the Finance Minister of India in his letter dated November 11, 1991, addressed to the President of the World Bank. The Finance Minister of India has assured the World Bank that the performance of the Indian economy shall be monitored in close coordination with the IMF/World Bank. This clearly means that a country of the size and stature of India, with a population of 840 million people, will have no control over her economic destiny. This is a fairly abrasive example of economic colonialism which is practiced by the rich nations through a subtle mechanism of providing loans under their principles of:

1. *Devaluation of the currency.* As per this principle, the currency of India has already been devalued by about 20 per cent in 1991. This means that the amount of debt owed by India to the western moneylenders automatically increases by the same 20 per cent amount in terms of Indian currency.
2. *Deregulation of the Industry.* As per this principle, the control of the State over the economy is deregulated. This clears the way for the multinational corporations to freely set up business in the country at their will where they could easily produce and sell goods not required by the majority of the population on the one hand and repatriate profits on the other, defying the criteria of equity and social justice for the large majority of the impoverished population.

In 1993 the GATT finalized its negotiations of various trade rules and regulations to be accepted by the world community. The Government of India, despite tremendous opposition to various rules, as finalized by GATT's former Director General Mr. Dunkel, has accepted the draft agreement, and regulations, which are detrimental to India, particularly those, related to drugs and agriculture industries. The Government of India agreed to sign the discriminatory GATT agreement under pressure from the World Bank and IMF combine. Madhu Dandavate[35], former Finance Minister of India, noted the following regarding the GATT agreement which has been accepted by the Government of India:

> "The agreement finalized by GATT is a sad reminder of..."Might is Right". This can never be the motto of global bodies which aspire to build harmonious and congenial

relations between various regions of the tension ridden World on the basis of justice and equity. In the GATT documents one sees neither the liberal ethos nor the far-sighted vision of Willy Brandt, who produced the monumental Brandt Commission Report on International Development issues."

L.K. Advani, a noted political leader of India, remarked[36]:

"Our party is committed to liberalization. But there is a Government that talks of liberalization in a manner so as to make our entire economic approach subject to the dictates of the IMF and the World Bank. "

The Government of India's recent moves for privatization of the economy under pressure from the IMF and the World Bank combine, without considering the special socio-economic ground realities of the Indian society, are not likely to become a panacea for the ills of the Indian economy. Even the Human Development Report 1993, as published by the United Nations Development Programmes (UNDP), cautioned against this privatization[37]:

"Privatization, conceived as one element of a total package, can stimulate private enterprise. Unfortunately, the process in many countries has been very different from this—more a "garage sale" of public enterprises to favoured individuals and groups than an integral part of a coherent strategy to encourage private investment.

Privatization in developing countries has therefore had very mixed results. In some cases, as in Mexico, it has been part of a process of fundamentally altering the organization of production—with benefits for consumers and the economy as a whole. In too many cases, however, privatization has taken place for the wrong reasons, under the wrong conditions and in the wrong way. Many countries seem to have been committing one or more of the seven deadly sins of privatization:

Don't only maximize revenue—create a competitive environment.

Don't replace public monopolies with private monopolies.

Don't sell through discretionary, non-transparent procedures, which invite allegations of corruption and nepotism.

Don't use sales proceeds to finance budget deficits—retire national debt.

Don't" crowd" financial markets with public borrowing at a time of public disinvestments.

Don't make false promises to labour—retrain them for new industries.

Don't rely merely on executive orders—create a political consensus."

Let us now look at the debt figures of India. Summed-up data for India from 1980 to 2001 are given in Table 2.18(A to G) in preceding Section B, which include Part (A) Foreign debt, (B) Interest paid, (C) Principal amount paid, (D) DSR, (E) Exchange rate of rupee, (F) Net outflow from India, and (G) Import-Export balance.

That Table 2.18(A to G) shows that an amount of Rs. 4,81,224 crore (approx. $ 100 billion) is outstanding as foreign debt in 2001 despite Rs. 72,558 crore paid as principal amount and Rs. 46,923 crore paid as interest during the decade of so called reforms that began in their enhanced form in 1991. New loans are now being negotiated just to pay principal and interest on earlier loans so as to keep those "old" loans as "current". The amount of interest of debt has been between Rs. 5,000 crore to Rs. 6,000 crore during most of the years of the socalled reforms since 1991. A.N. Roy[38] of the Institute of Social Sciences, New Delhi, pointed out that, *"for every $1 the West gives in aid to the developing countries, $9 comes back in debt service."*

The foreign debt of India is constantly on the rise from 1980 onwards till 2002 despite so much amount of principal and interest is constantly being paid every year since then. Since mid-1999s, despite all the assistance and all the loans from foreign countries, the net amount is being flown from out of India to the foreign lenders as shown in that Table 2.18(F), which is nearly Rs. 1,000 crore in 2000, and Rs. 3,000 crore in 2001.

The value of Dollar has risen six times against the Rupee during the twenty-year period from 1980 to 2001, i.e. from Rs. 7 in 1981 to Rs. 48 in 2001; and nearly three times during the ten year of reforms, i.e. from Rs. 17 in 1991 to Rs. 48 in 2001. The exports of India have also been falling short of imports during every year of these ten years of reforms from 1991 to 2001. During these ten years, imports at Rs.. 13,55,000 crore and exports at Rs. 11,39,000 crore, give a net shortage of exports at Rs. 2,16,000 (-ve).

The Debt Service Ratio (DSR) has certainly improved during this decade of reforms from 32.7 in 1991 to 15 in 2001 but at what cost to the people of India! The value of Rupee has nearly fallen three times during this decade of reforms from Rs. 17 in 1980 to Rs. 48 in 2001 and exorbitant amount of interest on foreign debt is being paid from securing the new loans! Is this a sign of a developing economy? Certainly not.

The above figures are discussed and put in Tables in Section B of this book, all taken from various Government of India documents and the World Bank.

These increases in the amount of debt, amount of interest, debt service ratio, and foreign exchange rate during the 10 years of so called reforms that began in 1991, indicate that India is fast heading towards a debt-trap of the type of Mexico and many Latin American countries during the 1990s, under the pressure of World Bank and the IMF combine.

This World Bank and the IMF combine is also controlling the speed and direction of the Indian economy, trying to turn India into a Banana Republic.

What used to be done by the Western powers during the colonial period by the direct political colonization of Asian, African and Latin American poor countries, is now being done through this IMF and the World Bank combine, after the disintegration of direct colonialism after the Second World War in 1945.The object of the Western powers during the direct political colonialism before the Second World War was to exploit the resources of the colonies, which is now being done through the remote control of the IMF and the World Bank combine.

With so much money being paid back to the developed nations through the World Bank and IMF combine, the poor countries are simply not left with bare necessary resources for the funding of their various socio-economic developmental projects. The huge interest on debts is a drain on the country's resources, not to mention the money repatriated by the multinational corporations of the Western countries.

A New York-based think-tank, North-South-Round-Table (NSRT), in its findings categorically stated in 1993 that the IMF and the World Bank have failed to provide social and economic security to most of the world's people, a situation which is still continuing even after ten years later in 2002.

## NOTES

1. *The Challenge to the South: The Report of the South Commission*, Oxford University Press, New York, 1990; p. 227.

   This Report was prepared under the chairmanship of Julius K. Nyerere and sanctioned by the Non-Aligned Movement (NAM) in 1986 in Zimbabwe. Dr. Man Mohan Singh, the Finance Minister of India since 1991, was one of the principal authors of this Report.
2. Kuldip Nayar, *Rajasthan Patrika* (Hindi Daily), Jaipur, 17.7.1991; p. 6. This passage of Nayar has been translated by the author from the original in Hindi. Nayar is an eminent journalist of India.
3. Ash Narain Roy, Join the war against debt, *Indian Express*, New Delhi, 11-10-2000 (Dak), p. 6. The writer is on the faculty of the Institute of Social Sciences, New Delhi.
4. Chapter 2(A) is an analysis of the situation from 1950 to 1970. The situation from 1970s to 1990s is discussed in Chapter 2(B).
5. A.M. Dambe, *Operation Canada Magazine*, Canadian International Development Agency (CIDA), Ottawa, Sept., Oct., 1973.
6. Julius K. Nyerere, *Freedom and Socialism*, (Dar-es-Salaam: Oxford University Press, 1968); p. 240.
7. *See* Sures Chandra Jain, *Indigenous Resources for Rural Development: Agricultural Mechanization and Rural Industrialisation*, Concept Publishing Company, New Delhi, 2004.

8. L.B. Pearson, *Partners in Development*, (New York: Praeger Pub., 1969); p. 175.
9. Teresa Hayter, *Aid as Imperialism*, (Middlesex, England: Penguin books, 1971); p. 174.
10. *See* Chapter 4, "International Development Agency".
11. Gunnar Myrdal, "Not only Aid", in L. Freedman and C. Cotter, (eds.). *Issues of the Sixties*, (Belmont, California: Wadswarth Pub., 1964); pp. 404-05.
12. Angelo Angelopolous, *The Third World and the Rich Countries*, (New York: Praeger Pub., 1972); p. 112.
13. L. Stepnoy, "The Problem of Economic Independence" in Y. Zhukov. *et al.*, (eds.) *The Third World*, (Moscow: Progress Publisher, 1970); p. 111.
14. See the statements of L.B. Pearson, President Julius K. Nyerere, and Dr. Martin Luther King, Jr., These have appeared as major quotations in Chapter 4.
15. L.B. Pearson, Partners in Development, *op. cit.*, pp. 95-96, emphasis in original.
16. *Ibid.* pp. 96-97, emphasis in original.
17. *See* New Internalist Magazine, Devo Press, Berkshire, England; May 1973; p. 1. After Independence, the name of Rhodesia has been changed to Zimbabwe.
18. Gunnar Myrdal, *The Challenge of World Poverty*, (New York: Pantheon Books, 1970); p. 351.
19. L.B. Pedson, *op. cit.*, p. 175.
20. Kristoffel Lieten, Multinationals and Development: Revisiting the Debate, in Frans J. Schuurman, Ed., *Globalization and Development Studies: Challenges for the 21st Century*, Vistaar Publications (A division of Sage Pub.), New Delhi, 2001, pp. 103, 113.
21. Willy Brandt, *North-South: A Programme for Survival*, (Cambridge: Mass, The MIT Press, 1980). This document is generally called the Brandt Commission Report. The so-called "Brandt Commission" is a group of intellectuals, called "Independent Commission on International Development Issues," headed by Willy Brandt, former Chancellor of the then West Germany.
22. *Ibid.*, pp. 290-91.
23. World Debt Tables, 1988-89, Vol. I, the World Bank, Washington DC, December, 1988; pp. X, XI.
24. Address by Barber B. Conable, President, the World Bank, Reuters Annual Lunchem, the Guildhall, London, April 27, 1989; p. 7.
25. Willy Brandt, *op. cit.*, p. 223.
26. Valentin Shehetinin, *Transnational Corporations*, (New Delhi: Allied Publishers, 1987); p. 132.

27. Arun Shourie, "The State As Personal Property," *The Economic and Political Weekly*, Bombay, March 8, 1980; p. 509.
28. Lester Bowles Pearson, *Pearson on Pearson Report*, CERES, FAO Review on Development, Rome, Italy, March-April 1970; pp. 20, 24.

    The "Pearson Report" is a document prepared under the Chairmanship of L.B. Pearson, former Prime Minister of Canada, a Nobel Laureate for Peace, to outline the strategies for the development of the Third World's poverty stricken people.

    This report was commissioned by the World Bank. The report is titled "Partners in Development", (New York: Praeger Pub., 1969).
29. This statement was made in the Arusha Declaration. Julius K. Nyerere, *Freedom and Socialism*, (Dar es Salaam: Oxford Univ. Press, 1968); p. 240.
30. *The Challenge to the South: The Report of the South Commission*, (New York: Oxford Univ. Press, 1990); pp. 227-29.
31. Data condensed from World Debt Tables, Vol. I, 1992-93, The World Bank, Washington DC, 1992; p. 160.
32. Altaf Gauher, *Indian Express*, New Delhi; 8-2-1987.
33. *The Hindustan Times*, New Delhi, 17-2-1992; p. 4.
34. *The Economic Times*, New Delhi, 27-2-1992; p. 3. There is tremendous coverage on this topic on pp. 1, 3 and 7 of this issue of *Economic Times*.
35. *Indian Express*, New Delhi, 3-1-1994; p. 8. For details on Brandt Commission Report as cited by Mr. Madhu Dandavate, see footnotes 1 & 2 of this chapter.
36. *Economic Times*, New Delhi, 10-8-1993, p. 2. In this article in the *Economic Times*, L.K. Advani has expressed had views on a wide range of issues dealing with the liberalization on Indian economy.
37. *Human Development Report, 1993*, United Nations Development Programme (UNDP), New York, 1993; pp. 49-50.
38. Ash Narain Roy, Join the war against debt, *Indian Express*, New Delhi, 11-10-2000 (Dak), p. 6.

# 3

# The Expenditures on Armament and Arms Imports *vs.* Health and Education

*... Arms are often a prime source of external debt. Military debt accounts for a third or more of total debt service in several large developing countries.*

—*Barbar Conable*[1], *1989*

*...South Asian governments have spent only $12 billion on education during 1990-96 while committing approximately $70 billion to defense.*

—*Human Development in South Asia*[2], *1998*

*"Many countries in Asia and Africa have not yet reached the standards that South Korea and reached in the mid-1950s. Progress, particularly since the 1980s, has been hampered by the withdrawal of money from human development expenditure to cover debt repayment... As an additional disconcerting variable, moderate to severe debt has touched virtually all developing countries. The unprecedented flow of resources from the developing countries into the core around the turn of the century into as even more painful, slower, lopsided and chaotic process it otherwise already would have been."*

—*Kristoffel Lieten*[3], *2001*

To study war and the reasons for its breakout with a view to curb further occurrences, we have to approach it dialectally rather than considering only its physical and material aspects, or its political nature and the subsequent leverage used to gain bargaining powers. It is essential to avoid the subjective and metaphysical nature of war in order to study its origins and causes. Further, to make a distinction and thorough analysis between a just and an unjust war in its historical perspective, a dialectical approach is imperative.

In general, as far as I can see all the wars subsequent to Second World War, have been fought, not with a view to gain territories or the resources of the enemy, but solely for economic reasons or on the ideological paradigms. Both the parties engaged in these wars, whether in Korea or Indo-China, Middle East and Israel, the Indian subcontinent or the Indo-Chinese conflict in 1962, faced the same terrible problem that of feeding the hungry masses and providing shelter, clothing and the adequate facilities for mass education. The giant colonialists before Second World War, with their shattered economies could no longer hold the political rein of the colonies. The disintegration of their colonial 'empire' gave birth to the newly independent States. But, unfortunately, the colonialists did their best to divide these nations to meet their selfish ends. Their tactic was simply to let these newly emerged States fight each other and then, and only then, could those nations be controlled economically. This trend still continues. The colonized nations have obtained their political independence, but economically all the former colonies are controlled by the economies of the developed nations. This is another form of colonialism, which is called neo-colonialism. These tactics have been successful in Korea, for North and South Korea always keep tension on their borders. The former colonialists have been successful in Indo-China for the same reasons. They have also been most successful on the Indian subcontinent, because here the former colonialists did not have to sacrifice their armed personnel, while in Korea and in Indo-China they did. Finally, these tactics have been used very successfully in the Middle East to date. Unfortunately for these former colonialists, their these nasty tactics did not work in China under Mao tse-Tung who took care of these former colonialists and who never miss an opportunity to establish their neo-colonialism.

When war-like hostilities or actual war itself breaks out, all the standards of morality, and even international relations, and the normally exercised courtesies are put at stake, at least during the war and for quite a while thereafter. During this period, only the brutal and barbaric law of jungle, 'might is right' prevails. This 'might' of the warring nations holds 'right' as long as the war material is supplied by the 'super powers' to meet their own selfish political and economical interests. All the wars subsequent to World War II have been fought only on the ideological conflicts to meet these selfish interests, or to maintain the influence of the 'super powers'. These wars can never be defined in terms of socio-cultural values, or to gain territory, or the material of the other party. These wars cannot be defined even in terms of biological, psychological, or natural aspects, because these wars have been carefully pre-planned and 'enough' war material is being supplied by the 'super powers' to keep these poor nations busy for only a few days or a week or two. For a poor nation, where average per capita income ranges from $ 80 to about $ 200 per year, (while in the developed nations it ranges from $ 3,000 to about $ 10,000), to be at war for even two weeks means a catastrophic economic setback at least for a few years to come. The harsh fact is that these poor nations remain poor for years after political independence.

We have to acknowledge the realities of these ideological conflicts, which result in the waging of wars. For peaceful coexistence and to avoid further recurrence, it is necessary to review and analyze dialectically the objective nature of the war and the motivations behind it, whatever they might be—political, economical, or ideological. This dialectical approach is necessary and is expected on the part of both the conflicting parties, and must be without any external pressure if a meaningful and a lasting settlement is to be achieved.

I now would like to review the 'development assistance' received by the underdeveloped nations and their military expenditures. As mentioned earlier, these nations have the military expenditures thrust upon them because of the division of their unity; Korea—north and south; Vietnam[4]—north and south; Indian[5] subcontinent—India, Pakistan and Bangladesh. The underdeveloped nations play a lesser role in the arms race on a global level[6]:

> "About 6 per cent of the total world military spending, and their influence on the world trend in expenditure and on the technological arms is minimal. ...To the citizens of a developing country, with a per capita income of about $ 200 a year, even the diversion of a few dollars for military purposes may rob him of one of the necessities of life."[7]

Table 3.1 shows that the group of developing nations, in 1970, (footnote b, in Table 3.1) received $ 1.3 billion (2.4 per cent of GNP) in 'development assistance' and they spent $ 7.2 billion (13.4 per cent of GNP) for military purposes. Around 1980, the developing nations are receiving about $ 20 billion annually in official aid[8]. In 1978 alone, the Third World imported about $ 14 billion of arms[9], in conventional weapons. About 70 per cent of the Arms to the Third World came from the USA ($ 5.8 billion), the USSR ($ 4.0 billion), the UK ($ 660 million) and Italy ($ 620 million).

Of the total military expenditure in the world in early 1980, over 80 per cent was borne by the two superpowers, the USA and the erstwhile USSR, as reported by the former Secretary General of the United Nations, Dr. Kurt Waldheim, at the beginning of the General Assembly's Special Session.[10] Disarmament held on June 7, 1982, in New York an appalling $ 1 million-a-minute of the day- and-night, or $ 525.6 billion a year. Now, during the 1990s, the amount of aid given by developed countries to developing countries is continuously diminishing. But the expenditure on arms purchase has almost doubled in just a decade from 1980 to 1990. The World Bank, in its annual World Development Report, 1991[11], noted that:

> "The world spends $ 1,000 billion on the military every year. In the late 1980s, military expenditure totalled $ 860 billion a year in high-income countries and $ 170 billion a year in developing ones. Of this $ 170 billion, $ 38 billion was spent on imports of arms, mostly from industrial countries.
>
> If global military expenditure were reduced, the world would undoubtedly be a better place. But is this realistic?"

**Table 3.1:** Developing Countries, 1970

| *Group of developing countries classed by Military expenditure as percentage of GNP* | *Number of countries* | *Population (million)* | *GNP ($ billions)* | *Military expenditure* | | *Bilateral official development assistance received* | |
|---|---|---|---|---|---|---|---|
| | | | | *$ billions* | *% of GNP* | *$ billions* | *% of GNP* |
| (1) | (2) | (3) | (4) | (5) | (6) | (7) | (8) |
| 5 and over | 17 | 219 | 54 | 7.2 | 13.4 | 1.3 | 2.4 |
| 2.5 to 4.9 | 18 | 1,012 | 151 | 5.0 | 3.3 | 2.6 | 1.7 |
| Under 2.5 | 46 | 428 | 136 | 2.0 | 1.5 | 1.3 | 0.9 |
| Total | 81 | 1,659 | 341 | 14.2 | 4.2 | 5.2 | 1.5 |

*Source:* Disarmament and Development, United Nations, New York, 1972, Table 2, p. 28, Document No. ST/ECA/174.

Out of this expenditure on armament and arms imports, the share of India, Pakistan and China is given in Table 3.2.

**Table 3.2:** Expenditure on Armaments and Arms Imports—India, Pakistan and China—1980-84 and 1985-89

| *Year* | *India* | *Pakistan* | *China* |
|---|---|---|---|
| 1980-84 | 7.375 | 1.980 | 19.80 |
| 1985-89 | 16.2 | 2.375 | 22.3 |

*Source:* Data condensed from an article by Dilip Mukerjee, *The Economic Times*, New Delhi, 18-3-1992; p. 6.

Of the total expenditure on military and arms in South Asia, India bears the brunt. While India bears 68.3 per cent, Pakistan bears 25.2 per cent the budget of India for 2002-03 is Rs. 65000 crore, which is about 2.5 per cent of the GDP.

India's military expenditure for 1995 to 1999 is given in Table 3.3.

**Table 3.3:** India's Military Expenditure from 1985 to 1999

*(Figures are in rupees billion)*

| *1995* | *1996* | *1997* | *1998* | 1999 |
|---|---|---|---|---|
| In local currency, at current prices | | | | |
| 260 | 288 | 338 | 397 | 450 |
| In constant US dollars | | | | |
| 8004 | 8165 | 8935 | 9264 | 10174 |
| As a share (%) of GDP | | | | |
| 2.1 | 2 | 2.2 | 2.1 | NA |

*Source:* Arnab Mitra, Arms & the men, *Economic Times*, New Delhi, 17-4-2000, p. 4.

The military burden in countries in South Asia in terms of Human advance and Human distress is given in Fig. 3.1 which shows that:

| *Human Advance* | *Human Distress* |
|---|---|
| **South Asia** | |
| There has been a noticeable improvement in the balance between military spending and social spending, the ratio having fallen from 113 per cent in 1960 to 72 per cent in 1990-91. | Global military spending decreased 6% annually between 1987-94, whereas it actually went up in South Asia by 1.6 per cent a year in real terms. While the rich industrial nations reduced the size of their armed forces by 24 per cent between 1987 and 1994, the poor South Asian countries increased their armed forces by 7.5 per cent during the same period. |
| **India** | |
| India spends 50 per cent more on education and health compared to its expenditure on defence. | India was ranked first in arms imports but ranked 142 in per capita income between 1988 and 1992. |
| **Pakistan** | |
| There has been a significant reduction of the gap between military spending and social spending during the last three decades, from nearly four times to one and one-quarter times. | There are nine soldiers for every one doctor and three soldiers for every two teachers. |
| **Bangladesh** | |
| There are three times more teachers than soldiers, the highest ratio in South Asia. | Military holdings (total military equipment of all descriptions) have gone up by 122 per cent in less than a decade. |
| **Nepal** | |
| Defence expenditure (as % of GNP) was only 1.1 per cent, the lowest in the region. | There are more soldiers (35) per doctor in Nepal than in any other country in the region. |
| **Sri Lanka** | |
| There are five teachers for every two soldiers, reflecting a strong national priority for education. | Defence expenditure has nearly doubled (in million US$) in less than a decade, increasing from 2.7 per cent of GDP in 1985 to 4.7 per cent in 1994. Military spending has increased by nearly 10 per cent a year during this period, compared to a global decline of 6 per cent a year. |

*Source:* Mahbub ul Haq, *Human Development in South Asia, 1997*, Oxford University Press, Karachi, Pakistan, 1997 (Details summarized from many pages).

**Fig. 3.1:** Military Burden

> Global military spending decreased 6 per cent annually between 1987-94, whereas it actually went up in South Asia by 1.6 per cent a year in real terms. While the rich industrial nations reduced the size of their armed forces by 24 per cent between 1987 and 1994, the poor South Asian countries increased their armed forces by 7.5 per cent during the same period.

The war machine of India and Pakistan includes large number of troops, tanks, artillery, combat aircraft, nuclear weapons and submarines, as shown in Table 3.4. With hostilities between India and Pakistan not going to retard as has been the situation of last decades, this regions of South Asia has emerged as one of the most militarized region of the World as reported by eminent economist and statesman of Pakistan, late Dr. Mahbub ul Haq[12] in Human Development in South Asia 1997:

> The current levels of military spending in South Asia are disturbing. While the region contains nearly 40 per cent of the world's poor, it also manages to spend around $14 billion a year on the military.
>
> It is evident that the level of military spending in India and Pakistan is largely independent of their low-income levels. In fact, the World Bank ranked India at 142 in terms of real per capita income (PPP dollars) between 1988 and 1992, yet it ranks first in the world in total arms imports. Pakistan's position is marginally better, at 119 in per capita income and tenth in arms imports. When most basic social services are missing in both India and Pakistan, as analyzed in Chapters 1 and 2, the rising defence burdens in these countries continue to impose prohibitive social and economic costs on their people. Defence expenditure exceeds spending on education and health in Pakistan by about a quarter. In India, defense spending consumes two-thirds as much resources as does combined spending on education and health. On the other hand, the rich industrial countries spend three times as much on education and health as on their military.

What is even more disturbing is the fact that South Asia is moving totally against global trends. Global military spending declined by about 37 per cent during the period 1987-94, from a peak of $1200 billion in 1987 to around $800 billion in 1994 (in 1993 prices). However, military spending in South Asia during the same period went up by 12 per cent, from $12.5 billion in 1987 to $14 billion in 1994, while it declined by 41 per cent in the industrial world, and by 13 per cent in the developing world.

**Table 3.4:** War Machine of India and Pakistan

| *Man/Equipment* | | *India* | *Pakistan* |
|---|---|---|---|
| *Troops:* | Active | 1.263 million | 620,000 |
| | Reserve | 535,000 | 513,000 |
| Tanks | | 3,414 | 2,300 |
| Artillery | | 4175 | 1467 |
| Air Force combat aircraft | | 738 | 353 |
| Air Force armed helicopters | | 22 | none |
| Nuclear weapons | | 66-90 | about 12 |
| Aircraft carriers | | 1 | none |
| Submarines | | 16 | 10 |

*Source:* Kanwar Sandhu, Can India's war machine deliver the killer punch? *Hindustan Times*, New Delhi, January 10, 2002, p. 9, (International Institute of Strategic Studies).

This is a pathetic situation that countries which are amongst the poorest in the World, are involved in armed conflict[13]:

Total world military expenditure rose 2.1 per cent in real terms in 1999 after a long period of decline ... The United States, Russia, China and France accounted for most of the global increase but countries spending relatively the most on guns are the emerging economies... *Arms spending totalled about $780 billion in 1999.* ...The countries with the heaviest economic burden on military expenditure are generally poor countries involved in armed conflict and/ or located in areas of tension."

Being involved in armed conflict with Pakistan, India has to bear substantial amount on arms[14]:

The annual defense expenditure (DE) for the financial year 2002-03 has been budgeted at Rs. 65,000 crore. ...The US defence outlay is to be increased by a staggering $48 billion—that will take it to $379 billion. A steady increase has been planned so that the defence tab peaks at $451 billion in 2007. Thus the increase of $48 billion is greater that the defense budget of the second largest spender, Japan which spends $46 billion. India incidentally spends under the equivalent of $135 billion annually—about 2.5 per cent of the GDP on defence.

A Congressional Research Service (CRS) Report of the US Congress, entitled Conventional Arms Transfer to the Third World—1983-90, lists India among the top 10 Third World arms importers in the world. During the period 1983-90, arms imported by the Third World countries are given in Table 3.5.

**Table 3.5:** Arms Imports by the Third World Countries in 1983-90

| | | *(US$ billions)* |
|---|---|---|
| 1. | Saudi Arabia | 48.1 |
| 2. | Iraq | 39.5 |
| 3. | India | 21.2 |
| 4. | Iran | 14.4 |
| 5. | Afghanistan | 14.3 |
| 6. | Syria | 13.7 |
| 7. | Cuba | 12.5 |
| 8. | Vietnam | 12.3 |
| 9. | Egypt | 9.7 |
| 10. | Libya | 9.6 |

*Source: The Hindustan Times*, New Delhi, August 13, 1991, p. 12.

Congressional Research Service (CRS) of the US Congress, entitled, Conventional Arms transfer to the Third World, 1983-90.

The aid is less than 1 per cent of GNP of the donor countries. As far as the contribution of aid is concerned, it is a well-established fact all over the world that aid-givers aided the developing countries not as much on humanitarian grounds as on feeding their own political ends. The World Bank, in its annual World Development Report, 1991[15] stated that:

> "Aid is sometimes turned on and off in response to the political and strategic agenda of bilateral funding agencies, making resource flows unpredictable. This resource instability can result in interruptions in development programmes, as in Egypt, India and Pakistan."

It is sickening to imagine the madness of expenditures on armament and arms imports. Just imagine that only a fraction of the money that the world spends on armament will be more than sufficient to provide food, education, and health and farm equipment. This has been stated by no less a person than Willy Brandt, the Nobel prize winner for Peace and former Chancellor of the then West Germany, in his capacity as Chairman of the independent Commission on International Development Issues, in his much publicized Report published in 1980, entitled: *North-South: A Programme for Survival*[16]:

"1. The military expenditure of only half a day would suffice to finance the whole malaria eradication programme of the World Health Organization, and less would be needed to conquer river-blindness, which is still the scourge of millions.
2. A modern tank costs about one million dollars, that amount could improve storage facilities for 100,000 tons of rice and thus save 4000 tons or more annually: one person can live on just over a pound of rice a day. The same sum of money could provide 1000 classrooms for 30,000 children.
3. For the price of one jet fighter (20 million dollars) one could set up about 40,000 village pharmacies.
4. One-half of one per cent of one year's world military expenditure would pay for all the farm equipments needed to increase food production and approach self-sufficiency in food-deficit low-income countries by 1990."

Cilla Ungerth[17] of UNESCO in Paris stated that the cost of providing education for all by the 2000 is equivalent to one week's military spending in the developing world or two days in the developed world, of what is being spent on armament in the world annually in the early 1990s.

If we compare the expenditure on military with official development assistance, it is noticed that the developing countries received about 5 per cent as official development assistance of what they spent on armament and arms imports.

Table 3.6 gives details on:

1. Military expenditure as percentage of GDP for 1990;
2. Military expenditure as percentage of combined education and health expenditures for the year 1990;
3. Annual average imports of major conventional arms by the various groups of developing countries as well as developed (industrial) countries.

Let us now review Table 3.7 for India and its pattern of expenditure on health, education, rural development and defence.

From these figures in Tables 3.6 and 3.7, it is seen that in India's, with her nearly 840 million people in 1991, the money spent on defence is nearly four times that of combined expenditures on health, education and rural development, Yet, given the perception of threats at India's border right from China's invasion in 1962 and Pakistan's attack in 1965, and the growing unrest within the country since early 1980s, it is not possible to cut down the expenditure on defence without risking the security of the country itself. Lt. Gen. S.K. Sinha[18] (Retd.) said:

> "Today (in 1991) we face a sinister combination of external threats which have got dovetailed with some growing internal dangers, the like of which has never been faced by us before. In the present sensitive security invironment, the slashing of the Defence budget to achieve economy can be disastrous. Compared to the outlay on Defence by other

**Table 3.6:** Military Expenditure and Resource use Imbalances

| | Military Expenditure (as % of GDP) | | Military Expenditure (as% of Combined Education and Health Expenditure) | | ODA given (as % of Military Expenditure) 1991 | Armed Forces | | | Annual Average Imports of Major Conventional Areas | |
|---|---|---|---|---|---|---|---|---|---|---|
| | 1960 | 1990 | 1977 | 1990 | | As % of Total Population 1987 | Per Teacher 1987 | Per Doctor 1987 | US$ Millions 1987–91 | As % of National Imports 1990 |
| (1) | (2) | (3) | (4) | (5) | (6) | (7) | (8) | (9) | (10) | (11) |
| *Developing Countries* | | | | | | | | | | |
| High human development | 1.9 | 2.5 | 96 | – | | 0.60 | 0.8 | 6 | 1,930 | 1.0 |
| Medium Human development | 6.9 | 3.7 | 86 | 230 | | 0.50 | 0.6 | 9 | 11,280 | 3.1 |
| Excluding China | 2.6 | 3.7 | 80 | – | | 0.70 | 0.9 | 15 | 11,120 | 3.7 |
| All developing countries | 4.2 | 3.4 | 91 | 169 | | 0.40 | 0.6 | 18 | 21,330 | 3.1 |
| Least developing countries | 2.1 | 2.8 | 89 | 146 | | 0.30 | 1.1 | 77 | 2,260 | 3.3 |
| Sub-Saharan Africa | 0.7 | 3.8 | 86 | 108 | | 0.20 | 0.9 | 76 | 1,180 | 2.6 |
| Industrial countries | 6.3 | – | – | – | | 0.80 | 1.0 | 3 | – | – |
| World | 6.0 | – | – | – | | 0.50 | 0.7 | 15 | – | – |

(*Contd.*)

(*Contd.*)

| (1) | (2) | (3) | (4) | (5) | (6) | (7) | (8) | (9) | (10) | (11) |
|---|---|---|---|---|---|---|---|---|---|---|
| *Industrially Developed Countries* | | | | | | | | | | |
| Industrial | 6.3 | – | – | – | – | – | 1.0 | 3.4 | – | – |
| Developing | 4.2 | 3.4 | 91 | 169 | – | 0.4 | 0.6 | 18.0 | – | – |
| World | 6.0 | – | – | – | – | – | 0.7 | 14.7 | – | – |
| OECD | 6.4 | 3.4 | 43 | 28 | 12.0 | 0.70 | 0.8 | 3.3 | 9,290 | – |
| Eastern Europe incl. former USSR | – | – | – | – | – | – | 1.4 | 3.6 | – | – |
| European Community | 4.7 | 2.9 | 36 | 27 | 18.6 | 0.80 | 0.9 | 3.8 | 4,330 | – |
| Nordic | 2.7 | 2.5 | 20 | 17 | 46.3 | 0.74 | 0.7 | 3.0 | 200 | – |
| Southern Europe | 3.3 | 2.2 | 39 | 29 | 17.6 | 0.86 | 1.0 | 4.7 | 410 | – |
| Non–Europe | 7.5 | 3.8 | 50 | 29 | 7.7 | 0.66 | 0.7 | 3.0 | 49,302 | – |
| North America | 8.5 | 5.3 | 53 | 32 | 4.4 | 0.83 | 0.9 | 3.6 | 4,730 | – |

*Source:* Data condensed from various tables from *Human Development Report, 1993*, The United Nations Development Programme, New York, 1993; pp. 176, 177 and 205.

developing and developed countries, our Defence spending is modest."

**Table 3.7:** Expenditure in India on Health, Education, Rural Development and Defence in 1991-92 and 1992-93

(*Rs. in crores*)

| | *1991-92* | *1992-93* |
|---|---|---|
| Total Expenditure | 113102 | 119086 |
| On Education | 903 | 951 |
| On Health | 281 | 302 |
| On Rural Development | 2304 | 2532 |
| On Defence | 16350 | 17500 |

*Source:* Data summarized from various Government of India's public documents.

Defence Expenditure as per cent of GNP, Military Expenditure as per cent of Health Education, Foreign Debt, Debt Service Ratio, Defence Expenditure, for 2000 are shown in Table 3.8.

Burden of military expenditure in countries in South Asia as per cent of GDP, as per cent of Central Government expenditure, and as per cent of education and health spending are given in Table 3.9.

Total external debt, military expenditure per cent of GNP, public expenditure on education and health of the various regions of the world for 2000 are given in Table 3.10.

Military/Social Spending ratio in South Asian Countries for 1990-91 are given in Table 3.11.

So there is a real problem here. Resources are required for the minimum up-lift of more than 80 per cent of the people, and yet we must continue to spend on arms race.

The expenditures on arms and defence of the developing countries continue to rise. The former World Bank president, Barber Coinable, in his address to the opening session of the annual meeting of the World Bank and the IMF, September 26, 1989, in Washington, revealed that developing countries spent nearly US $ 200 billion on military and armament. Out of a total foreign debt of US $ 1300 billion of developing countries, the World Bank President revealed also that[19]:

**Table 3.8:** Defence Expenditure as per cent of GNP, Military Expenditure as per cent of Health Education, Foreign Debt, Debt Service Ratio, Defence Expenditure for 2000

| *Country Region* | *Defence exp. as % of GNP 1995* | *% Share of Military Exp. in South Asia 1991* | *Military/ Social Spending Ratio 1990-91 South Asia* | *Defence exp. (as % of Govt. Exp.) 1995* | *Defence Exp. (as % of Education and Health) 1991* | *External Debt 1998 (US$, billion)* | *DSR 1998* | *Defence Exp. US$ millions 1995* |
|---|---|---|---|---|---|---|---|---|
| | *HDSA 98 p 184* | *HDSA 97 p 82* | *HDSA 97 p 82* | *HDSA 98 p 184* | *HDSA 98 p 184* | *WDR p 315* | *HDR p 219* | *HDSA 98 p 184* |
| India | 2.8 | 68.3 | 65 | 14.5 | 65 | 98.2 | 20.6 | 9,360 |
| Pakistan | 5.2 | 25.2 | 125 | 26.9 | 125 | 32.2 | 23.6 | 2,900 |
| Bangladesh | 1.4 | 2.7 | 41 | 17.6 | 41 | 16.4 | 9.1 | 400 |
| Nepal | 0.9 | 0.2 | 35 | 5.9 | 35 | 2.6 | 7.0 | 40 |
| Sri Lanka | 5.3 | 3.6 | 107 | 2.6 | 107 | 8.5 | 6.6 | 670 |
| Bhutan | — | — | — | n/a | n/a | 0.120 | 6.3 | n/a |
| Maldives | — | — | — | n/a | n/a | 0.18 | 3.1 | n/a |
| South Asia | 3.4 | — | — | 16.7 | 72 | 172.7 | 18.9 | 13,370 |

*Sources:* Data extracted from:

(1) Mahbub ul Haq and Khadija Haq, Human Development in South Asia 1997, The Human Development Centre, Karachi, Pakistan, (Oxford University Press, Karachi, Pakistan, 1997).
(2) Mahbub ul Haq and Khadija Haq, Human Development in South Asia 1998, The Human Development Centre, Karachi, Pakistan, (Oxford University Press, Karachi, Pakistan, 1998).
(3) United Nations Development Programme, Human Development Report, 2000, (Oxford University Press, New York, 2000).
(4) The World Bank, World Development Report, 2000/2001, (Oxford University Press, New York, 2000).

**Table 3.9:** Burden of Military Expenditure in South Asia

| *Sl. No.* | *Country* | *As % of GDP* | | *As % of central govt. expenditure* | | *As % of education and health spending* | |
|---|---|---|---|---|---|---|---|
| | | *1985* | *1994* | *1980* | *1994* | *1985* | *1990-91* |
| 1. | Bangladesh | 1.3 | 1.5 | 9.4 | 1.6 | n/a | 41 |
| 2. | Bhutan | n/a | n/a | n/a | n/a | n/a | n/a |
| 3. | India | 2.6 | 3.6 | 14.1 | 12.8 | 68 | 65 |
| 4. | Maldives | n/a | n/a | n/a | n/a | n/a | n/a |
| 5. | Nepal | 0.8 | 1.1 | 6.1 | 5.9 | 67 | 35 |
| 6. | Pakistan | 5.2 | 7.0 | 30.6 | 26.9 | 393 | 125 |
| 7. | Sri Lanka | 2.7 | 4.7 | 1.6 | 11.6 | 17 | 107 |
| *8.* | *Average South Asia* | 2.4 | 3.4 | *15.1* | *14.7* | *113* | 72 |
| | *Memo Items* | | | | | | |
| 9. | World | 4.3 | 3.2 | n/a | n/a | 104 | 37 |
| 10. | Developing Countries | 5.5 | 3.6 | n/a | n/a | 143 | 60 |
| 11. | Industrial Countries | 4.1 | 3.1 | n/a | n/a | 97 | 33 |
| 12. | East Asia (excl. China) | 7.4 | 4.8 | n/a | n/a | 273 | 49 |
| 13. | China | 7.9 | 5.6 | n/a | n/a | 387 | 114 |
| 14. | Sub-Saharan Africa | 2.1 | 2.9 | n/a | n/a | 27 | 43 |

*Source:* Mahbub ul Haq, *Human Development in South Asia, 1997,* Oxford University Press, Karachi, Pakistan, 1997, p . 80.

**Table 3.10:** External Debt, Military Expenditure per cent of GNP, Public Expenditure on Education and Health of the various regions of the World for 2000

| *Region* | *External Debt $ millions 1998* | *Military Expenditure % of GNP 1997* | *Public Expenditure on Education % of GNP 1997* | *Public Expenditure on Health % of GDP 1990-98* |
|---|---|---|---|---|
| | *WDR p 315* | *WDR p 307* | *WDR p 285* | *WDR p 287* |
| World | — | 2.5 | 4.8 | 2.5 |
| Low Income | 579,545 | 2.9 | 3.3 | 1.3 |
| Middle Income | 1,956,501 | 2.9 | 4.8 | 3.1 |
| Low and Middle Income | 2,536,046 | 2.9 | 4.1 | 1.9 |
| East Asia & Pacific | 667,522 | 2.5 | 2.9 | 1.7 |
| Europe and Central Asia | 480,539 | 4 | 5.1 | 4.0 |
| Latin America & Caribbean | 786,019 | 1.8 | 3.6 | 3.3 |
| Middle East & North Africa | 208,059 | 7.0 | 5.2 | 2.4 |
| South Asia | 163,775 | 3.1 | 3.1 | 0.8 |
| Sub-Saharan Africa | 230,132 | 2.3 | 4.1 | 1.5 |

*Source:* The World Bank, *World Development Report 2000/2001*, Oxford University Press, New York, 2000.

**Table 3.11:** Military/Social Spending Ratio (1990-91) in South Asian Countries

| *Country* | *Defence expenditure as a % of education and health expenditure* |
|---|---|
| Pakistan | 125 |
| Sri Lanka | 107 |
| India | 65 |
| Bangladesh | 41 |
| Nepal | 35 |

*Source:* Mahbub ul Haq and Khadija Haq, *Human Development in South Asia 1997*, The Human Development Centre, Karachi, Pakistan, (Oxford University Press, Karachi, Pakistan, 1997), p. 82.

"...Arms are often a prime source of external debt. Military debt accounts for a third or more of total debt service in several large developing countries."

There has been a growing concern in the United Nations for disarmament. Delegates have been raising their voice for disarmament pleading that the money saved from disarmament should be invested in developmental activities, particularly in the least developed countries. There have so far been three special sessions of the General Assembly of the United Nations on disarmament in 1978, 1982 and 1988. But the recommendations made in these special sessions have fallen on deaf ears. The arms race keeps going unabated.

The transformation of military expenditures into the development projects will certainly improve the socio-economic level of the poverty-stricken people in the Third World. This transformation of military expenditures into development projects will reduce the ever increasing gap between the economic status of the poor and the rich nations and will also lower the ratio of imports to NDP which is imperative for a policy of import substitution. Unfortunately, the production and stockpile of destructive weapons, especially the nuclear ones, in the present system of the socalled "balance of power", have become "stabilizing" factors on the pretext of maintaining international peace and security. It means that we can only be 'secure' under the constant fear of the outbreak of the nuclear war and "live each day on the verge of nuclear co-annihilation", as Dr. Martin Luther King[20], Jr. remarked. Is this not stupid enough? Is this not insanity? Does the development of the nuclear weapons by the Peoples Republic of China not indicate this very same "balance of power", where so much is still needed for economic development? Does the Indian nuclear explosion (though of relatively smaller size—about 15,000 TNT,.or equivalent to that which were dropped over Hiroshima and Nagasaki) not indicate the very same motives of the "balance of power"? Does the pledge by the former Prime Minister of Pakistan, Z.A. Bhutto[21], that, "We will eat leaves and grasses, even go hungry, but we will have to get one nuclear bomb of our own. We have no alternative," not indicate the domination of the same ideology? All this means that we have accepted the idea that first we will prepare ourselves for war to be "secure", and then we will take care of the bare necessities of life, while over three-fourths of the inhabitants of the earth suffer so desperately. Here, however, in this context we cannot afford to ignore that, if nuclear war breaks out, it will not only be the disaster of the economies of the nations involved but it would be a world tragedy because[22], "it will most certainly involve the use of nuclear missiles and would draw into its orbit many countries and nations."

The total money being spent on research and development of the world is about $ 60 billion[23] per year in 1970, or about 2 per cent of the world GNP; out of this about $ 25 billion alone, or about 41 per cent goes to military related research; only about $ 6 billion a year, or about 10 per cent goes to health-related research. This is certainly a crime against the majority of humanity. The military expenditure[24] in the 1960s was $ 120 billion annually on the average of the total world ($ 150 billion at the 1970 prices), in the 1970s, it is averaging about $ 200 billion a year. In the 1980s[25], the annual military expenditures continue to absorb their present percentage of world output: they are about 525.6 billion a year, over $ 1 million a minute of the day-and-night.

The economic scale of the current world military expenditures can be realized more dramatically when we remember that they all equal the combined GNP of UK and Italy, or that of the developing countries of South Asia, the Far East and Africa together, with a total population of 1300 million[26] in 1970. Having these figures in mind of what is being spent on military on one side, and the dire problems of hunger, shelter, clothing and illiteracy on the other it is the moral obligation of every sensible person to think about curbing the arms race and reducing military expenditures. This is in the interests of both the developed and the underdeveloped nations. The savings in the military expenditures of the developed nations will increase the possibility for providing additional aid[27] as well as increased trade on relatively favourable terms. The underdeveloped nations will find it relatively easy (in terms of scarce foreign exchange) to defray the initial outlay required for providing the necessary infrastructure upon which to build and execute the development projects. In addition to this, the natural resources, now being consumed by the manufacturing of the armaments, could well be utilized to fulfil the needs of so many people. Above all, in addition to all the economic benefits of disarmament, it is more imperative to curb the nuclear weapons because a human or technical error could be of devastating consequences. This is all the more important now in after of the break-up of the USSR. Nuclear armaments of the erstwhile USSR are now in the hands of 15 republics, in which the Republic of Russia retains the lion's share, about 70 per cent of the total nuclear armament of the erstwhile USSR.

With the end of the cold war between the USA and the erstwhile USSR, and the open willingness of the republic of Russia, the largest of old Soviet Union republics, historic opportunity has been thrown to the world community to drastically cut down the expenditure on armaments.

Both the President of the USA and the President of the Republic of Russia expressed their willingness[28] in January 92 to scrap the major weapon systems. The military budget of $ 285.9 of the USA for 1993 would be $ 8 billion less than agreed earlier. Robert McNamara, former president of the World Bank, recommended (1991) that[29]:

> "In the case of the United States...it should be possible within six to eight years to cut military spending by half in relation to Gross National Product (GNP), that is, from 6 per cent to 3 per cent.
>
> Similar reductions can be made in the military expenditures of Third World countries, which now total some $ 170 billion annually, or 4.3 per cent of their collective GNP."

This is first time in the post Second World War history since 1945 that there is a thinking of cut in the military budget of the USA. Boris Yeltsin[30], President of the Republic of Russia even went further and declared that:

> "Nuclear weapons and other mass destruction means of the world must be eliminated."

The late Dr. Martin Luther King[31], Jr., the civil right leader of the USA and a world statesman of the order of Mahatma Gandhi of India, had said in 1967 that:

> "We in the West must bear in mind that the poor countries are poor primarily because we have exploited them through political or economic colonialism."

Now with this fact in mind that the developing countries of the world are poor because they were exploited by the West during the colonial period prior to the Second World War, and now that the cold war has ended between the USA and the erstwhile USSR, the "saving" from the cut in military spending should be invested on the general up-lift of the developing countries.

Julius K. Nyerere, former president of Tanzania, and an internationally acknowledged spokesman of the cause of people in the Third World, published a Report in 1990 entitled *The Challenge to the South*—the Report of the South Commission, sanctioned by the Non-Aligned Movement (NAM) in 1986 in Zimbabwe, recommended that[32]:

> "The time has come therefore for effective multilateral action to scale down the debt and reduce the burden of debt service to tolerable levels. In most cases, the debt crisis has turned out to be a crisis of solvency rather than merely of liquidity.
>
> ...The upshot is that debt has become a form of bondage, and the indebted economies have become indentured economies—a clear manifestation of neo-colonialism. This state of affairs cannot go on. The debt and its service must be reduced to a level that allows growth to proceed at an acceptable pace.
>
> ...We reaffirm the need for an International Debt Conference with the participation of the debtor governments, the governments of the creditors, and the international financial institutions, whose mandate would be to arrive at a binding international agreement on a framework solution. The international financial institutions must

evolve a medium—term programme regarding the net financing needs of debtor countries consistent with the accepted growth objective. The international political community must assume its responsibility in this area."

Even before the ending of the cold war and the disintegration of the erstwhile USSR, Willy Brandt[33], former West German Chancellor and Nobel Laureate for Peace, in his internationally acclaimed report for the up-lift of the developing countries, published in 1980, entitled *North South—A Programme for Survival*, had recommended that:

"There must be a substantial increase in the transfer of resources to developing countries in order to finance:

1. Projects and programmes to alleviate poverty and to expand food production especially in the least developed countries.
2. Exploration and development of energy and mineral resources.
3. Stabilization of the prices and earnings of commodity exports and expanded domestic processing of commodities."

The political changes in the World have been sweeping since 1989. Communism is dead in the countries of Eastern Europe and erstwhile USSR. With communism buried in the books of history, East and West Germany have been united into a single State. Efforts are made to economically unite all the countries in Europe with a single currency, etc. This rapidly changing political environment of the world has been in the positive direction for international peace and security. With this positive international environment, if the leaders of the world community, particularly the USA and countries in Europe, heed the recommendations of the Brandt (1980) and Nyerere (1990) Reports, the world would be a better place to live in, both for developed and the developing countries. Under the new international environment, "the concept of human security must stress the security of people, not only of nations", as stated in the (United Nations Development

Programme) UNDP's Annual *Human Development Report, 1993*[34]:

> "The concept of security must change from an exclusive stress on national security to a much greater stress on peoples' security, from security through armaments to security through human development, from territorial security to food, employment and environmental security.
>
> The world has already made a good start:
>
> Global military expenditures have declined cumulatively by around $ 240 billion since 1987.
>
> Nuclear warheads will be cut by two-thirds by the year 2003 as a result of the recent US-Russia agreement.
>
> More than two million people have been demobilized from the armed forces since the beginning of the 1990s.
>
> Defence industries are expected to have cut nearly a fourth of their workforce by 1998.
>
> This is a beginning, but a formidable agenda still awaits policy-makers."

The recommendations of these UN reports largely remain of paper. The plight of the HIPs (highly indebted poor countries) continue to get from bad to worse, as reported in an Editorial of the *Hindustan Times*[35]:

> It is no secret that the debt burden is crippling the HIPCs' (Highly Indebted Poor Countries) efforts to sustain growth or to gain independence from the international financial institutions. While they have to spend 10 per cent of their income on health and education, about 60 per cent is going towards servicing of the debt. *...Heavily indebted poor countries (HIPCs)...are spending $ 60 million a day towards debt servicing.*

In the report of the Human Development in South Asia 1998, it was mentioned that[36]:

> "South Asian governments have spent only $12 billion on

education during 1990-96 while committing approximately $70 billion to defence."

Kristoffel Lieten[37] stated that:

"Many countries in Asia and Africa have not yet reached the standards that South Korea and reached in the mid-1950s. Progress, particularly since the 1980s, has been hampered by the withdrawal of money from human development expenditure to cover debt repayment...As an additional disconcerting variable, moderate to severe debt has touched virtually all developing countries. The unprecedented flow of resources from the developing countries into the core around the turn of the century into as even more painful, slower, lopsided and chaotic process it otherwise already would have been."

## NOTES

1. Barbar Conable, former president of the World Bank, Washington, DC, *Indian Express*, New Delhi, 27-9-89; p. 7.
2. Mahbub ul.Haq and Khadija Haq, *Human Development in South Asia 1998*, The Human Development Centre, Karachi, Pakistan, (Oxford University Press, Karachi, Pakistan, 1998, p. 6).
3. Kristoffel Lieten, Multinationals and Development: Revisiting the Debate, in Frans J. Schuurman, Ed., *Globalization and Development Studies: Challenges for the 21st Century*, Vistaar Publications (A division of Sage Pub.), New Delhi, 2001, pp. 103, 113.
4. Vietnam is the only nation in the post-Second World War era that was divided into North and South (as most of the nations have been, e.g. Germany, Indian subcontinent) by the imperialism of the Western powers, and has since been united again into one country. The corrupt dictatorial regime in South Vietnam, backed by unprecedented U.S. military machine and even over half a million U.S. service personnel, was defeated in 1975, by the Communist forces of North Viet Nam.
5. India was divided into India and Pakistan in 1947 and then Pakistan was divided into Pakistan and Bangladesh in 1971.
6. Consequences of the Arms Race and Military Expenditures, report of the Secretary-General of the United Nations, U. Thant, Economic and Social Council, United Nations, New York, 1972; p. 10.

7. Willy Brandt, former German Chancellor and Chairman of the International Commission on Development Issue, in collaboration with leading people from and around the world, published a book what has now come to be known as the Brandt Commission Report. It is titled *North-South: A Programme for Survival* (Cambridge, Mass.: The M.I.T. Press, 1980). In this report, Mr. Brandt outlined the compassionate situation of the millions of people in the Third World who are undernourished illiterate and do not have access to essential medical care.
8. *Ibid.*, p. 117.
9. *Ibid.*, p. 120.
10. In June 1982, a special session of the General Assembly of the United Nations was held in New York. This session was exclusively devoted the problems of arms race, especially the build-up of the nuclear arsenal, more than enough already to kill every human being on this planet seven times over. Peace-loving peoples throughout the World gathered in New York and protested outside the General Assembly of the United Nations where the meeting was being held.
11. *The World Development Report 1991*, The World Bank, Washington DC, 1991; p. 140.
12. Mahbub ul Haq, *Human Development in South Asia, 1997*, Oxford University Press, Karachi, Pakistan, 1997, pp. 97, 80.
13. SIPRI, World's arms expenditure rising, *Times of India*, New Delhi, 15-6-2000, p. 16.
14. C. Uday Bhaskar, Shore up Defenses, *Times of India*, New Delhi, 18-3-2002, p. 4.
15. *Ibid.*, p. 48.
16. Willy Brandt, *op. cit.*, p. 14.
17. *The Economic Times*, New Delhi, 3-9-1990; p. 9.
18. *Hindustan Times*, New Delhi, 12-2-1992; p. 13.
19. *The Indian Express*, New Delhi, 27-9-1989, p. 7.
20. Martin Luther King, Jr., *Conscience for Change*, (Toronto: Canadian Broadcasting Corporation, 1967); p. 37.
21. *Time Magazine*, Toronto, Canadian edition, June 3, 1974; p. 29. Mr. Bhutto was later overthrown in a military coup in 1977, led by Gen. Zia-ul-Haq, and subsequently sentenced to death, and hanged, in 1979, for allegedly conspiring to have his political opponents murdered in an armed ambush.
22. *Thermo-Nuclear War: The Greatest Crime Against Humanity*, (Moscow: Progress Pub., 1972); p. 96.
23. *Disarmament and Development*, New York: United Nations, 1972; p. 16.
24. *Conseuqneces of the Arms Race and of Military Expenditures*, report of the Secretary-General of the United Nations, New York, 1972; p. VIII.

25. Statement given by the Secretary-General of the United Nations, on June 7, 1982, in New York, on the occasion of inaugurating the special session of the General Assembly of the U.N., in New York, to discuss the problems of arms race, particularly the build-up of the nuclear arsenal.
26. *Consequences of the Arms Race and of Military Expenditures, op. cit.*, p. VIII.
27. A concise formulation of these relationships has been worked out by Wasily Leongief and some other members of the Group. The algebraic basis for the statement is made in paragraphs 33 and 34 is as follows. Let

    V : the cut in military expenditure expressed as a proportion of military expenditure before disarmament;

    W : the minimum necessary increase in assistance, taken as a proportion of the amount of assistance before disarmament, if the income gap is not to widen.

    M : military expenditures before disarmament.

    D : "disposable "GNP", i.e. total GNP less military expenditure less assistance, in the case of developed countries, and total GNP less military expenditure plus assistance, in the case of developing countries.

    A : assistance transferred from developed to developing countries, respectively.

    If the income gap is to remain constant

    D + MV – AW D2 + M2 – V + AW
    11– – = –
    ______________________________
    D1 D2

    Accordingly, the corresponding relationship between w and v can be achieved as follows:

    w = vM1 D2 – M2 D1
    ____________________
    A (D1 + D2)

    the co-efficient of v in this formula has a value of approximately unity when data for 1970 are inserted. If all data are expressed in per capita terms, the relationships presented above are the same.

    *Source: Disarmament and Development*, United Nations, New York, 1972, p. 13, para 34, (footnote 12).
28. *The Times of India*, New Delhi, 30-1-1992, p. 1.
29. *The Hindustan Times*, New Delhi, 6-5-1991, p. 13.
30. *The Times of India*, New Delhi, 30-1-1992, p. 1.
31. Martin Luther King, Jr., *Conscience for Change*, The Canadian Broadcasting Corporation, Toronto, 1967; p. 36.

32. *The Challenge to the South*: The Report of the South Commission, (New York: Oxford University Press, 1990); pp. 226-28.

    This Report, sanctioned by Non-Aligned Movement (NAM) in 1986 in Zimbabwe, was prepared by the South Commission under the chairmanship of the former president of Tanzania, Julius K. Nyerere.

    India's Dr. Man Mohan Singh, former Governor of the Reserve Bank of India, and Minister of Finance since 1991 was one of the principal authors of this Report. Dr. Man Mohan Singh in his capacity as Finance Minister of India since June 1991, is without doubt the single force, backed-up by the Prime Minister P.V. Narasimha Rao, of course, who has caused the foreign debt of India to become twice just in two years, from Rs. 1,28,451 crore in 1989-90 to Rs 2.,66,167 crore in 1991-92.

    This debt has doubled partly by borrowing heavily and partly by devaluing the Indian currency in 1991, at the behest of the IMF and the World Bank combine.
33. *North-South: A Programme for Survival*, (Cambridge: The MIT Press, 1980); p. 290.
34. *Human Development Report 1993*, The United Nations Development Programme (UNDP), New York, 1993; p. 2.
35. Editorial, Blessed are the poor, *Hindustan Times*, New Delhi, 25-7-2000, p. 15.
36. Mahbub ul Haq and Khadija Haq, *Human Development in South Asia 1998*, The Human Development Centre, Karachi, Pakistan, (Oxford University Press, Karachi, Pakistan, 1998), p. 6.
37. Kristoffel Lieten, Multinationals and Development: Revisiting the Debate, in Frans J. Schuurman, Ed., *Globalization and Development Studies: Challenges for the 21st Century*, Vistaar Publications (A division of Sage Pub.), New Delhi, 2001, pp. 103, 113.

# 4

# International Development Agencies: A Mechanism of Maintaining Status Quo

*"The transformation of relations between East and West has ended the Cold War, freeing minds and resources that for so long were bound by sterile confrontation.*

*We have historical opportunity to change the way we deal with the world's increasing interdependencies."*

*Ingvar Carlsson*[1]*, Julius Nyerere, and Willy Brandt, 1991*

The aids, loans, and private investment from developed nations fulfil only one part of the development equation, given by the former U.N. Secretary-General, U. Thant, "Development = Economic Growth + Social Change", and that part is the "Economic Growth", if at all. In the previous chapters, I tried to formulate some policy-generating systems (considering the socio-cultural value system of the recipient nations based upon mutual respect, peaceful coexistence, and sovereign rights of each other) among nations through unconditional international cooperation, within the framework of the UN Charter. The formulation the development strategies of the underdeveloped nations must see to it that 'developing' nations in a real sense can develop. Today, the reviews and appraisals indicate that we cannot use the term 'developing', for most of the underdeveloped nations which are not really 'developing' at all. Poverty, illiteracy, malnutrition continue to go down the bill in most of the nations.

The UNDP is the principal largest channel for multilateral and technical cooperation with, and pre-investment assistance to, the low-income countries. It is active on virtually every economic and social level. Pre-investment and technical assistance projects supported by the UNDP have two general and closely related aims. The first is to help low income countries create favourable conditions for mobilizing development capital on a sound and business like basis from both domestic and external sources. The second is to prepare a survey for fully effective use of such investment capital and all other economic and human resources that are available. In 1961, the General Assembly of the UN designated the 1960s as the UNDD-I. In 1971 UNDD-II was launched. Its main objective was to promote economic growth, especially in the developing countries, to ensure a higher standard of living consistent with human dignity, to bring about sustained improvement in the well being of the individual, and to facilitate the process of narrowing the ever-widening economic gap between the developed and developing countries.

The UNCTAD was established as a permanent organ of the General Assembly of the UN in December 1964. The main role of the UNCTAD, as formulated in its charter, is to promote international trade with a view to accelerate economic development, to formulate new principles and policies to this end, to negotiate multinational trade agreements and, generally, to act as a centre for harmonizing government policies and actions in the field of trade and related problems of development. We will now look at the goals set for the UNDD-I for the 1960s and for the UNDD-II for the 1970s, the resolutions and agreements reached after the lengthy meetings of UNCTAD (held in Geneva, March-June 1964; UNCTAD-II, held at New Delhi, February-March 1968; and the UNCTAD-III, held at Santiago, April-May 1972), and the goals set up in the UN International Development Strategy for the 1970s. The goals were set up, resolutions were passed, agreements were reached, and this was the end of the game. This is the way the UN agencies function! Is there any implementation of the resolutions and agreements to make an effective contribution to the development system for which they are passed? Bitterness and frustrations are created when "agreements and resolutions" are just "agreements and resolutions", without any significant implementation. Why are the resolutions not enforced? Why are the agreements not implemented? What are the reasons and causes behind this are inaction? What are the strategies behind not implementing the resolutions and agreements reached at the UN agencies involved in the process of development?

The question now arises: What is this global "interdependence" or the strategies behind not implementing the resolutions adopted at the international forms?

We notice that the following International Reports have been published from 1950s to 1990s regarding the development of the Third World:

1. For the 1950s[2]: The United Nations Development Decade-I. It failed miserably.
2. For the 1960s[3]: The United Nations Development Decade-II: It too failed. It did not achieve its stated objective.
3. For the 1970s[4]: Partners in Development, report of the Commission on International Development, commissioned by the World Bank, under the Chairmanship of L.B. Pearson, former Prime Minister of Canada, a Nobel laureate for Peace. Recommendations of this report were dead even before their scheduled review.
4. For the 1980s[5]: North-South—A Programme for Survival; report of the Independent Commission on International Development Issues, under the chairmanship of Willy Brandt, former Chancellor of West Germany and Nobel Prize winner for Peace.

   In the Brandt Commission Report, an emergency programme for the up-lift of the developing countries for 1980-85 was spelled out, none of which has ever been implemented, such as[6]

   "There must be substantial increase in the transfer of resources to developing countries in order to finance:

   1. Projects and programmes to alleviate poverty and

to expand food production, especially in the least developed countries.
2. Exploration and development of energy and mineral resources.
3. Stabilization of the prices and earnings of commodity exports and expanded domestic processing of commodities."

5. For the 1990s[7]: The Challenge to the South: The Report of the South Commission, under the chairmanship of Julius K. Nyerere, former President of Tanzania and internationally acclaimed authority on developmental issues in the Third World. The Non-Aligned Movement sanctioned this Report in 1986 in Zimbabwe. In this Report, while emphasis has been laid for cooperation within the developing world (i.e. the South, as mentioned in this Report) and with a request to the developed countries (i.e. the North as mentioned in this Report) to reduce the debt burden[8]:

   "The time has come therefore for effective multilateral action to scale down the debt and reduce the burden of debt service to tolerable levels. In most cases, the debt crisis has turned out to be a crisis of solvency rather than merely of liquidity. ...

   The upshot is that debt has become a form of bondage, and the indebted economies have become indentured economies—a clear manifestation of neo-colonialism. This state of affairs cannot go on. The debt and its service must be reduced to a level that allows growth to proceed at an acceptable pace.

   ...We reaffirm the need for an International Debt Conference with the participation of the debtor governments, the governments of the creditors, and the international financial institutions, whose mandate would be to arrive at a binding international agreement on a framework solution."
6. For the 2000s, the Millennium's first decade, United Nations Millennium Declaration.

The leaders of the World Community met at the United Nations and resolved to eradicate poverty from the face of Earth by 2015[9]:

### *The Millennium Declaration's Goals for Development and Poverty Eradication*

As the world entered the new millennium, heads of state and government gathered at the United Nations General Assembly to lay out their vision for the world. The leaders of the summit adopted the United Nations Millennium Declaration, recognizing their "collective responsibility to uphold the principles of human dignity, equality and equity at the global level". Among the many objectives set out by the declaration are specific, quantified and monitorable goals for development and poverty eradication by 2015:

- To halve the proportion of the world's people living on less than $1 a day.
- To halve the proportion of the world's people suffering from hunger.
- To halve the proportion of the world's people without access to safe drinking water.
- To achieve universal completion of primary schooling.
- To achieve gender equality in access to education.
- To reduce maternal mortality ratio by three quarters.
- To reduce under-five mortality rate by two-thirds.
- To halt and begin to reverse the spread of HIV/AIDS, malaria and other major diseases.

These goals build on the international development goals, which include three more targets—namely, to reduce infant mortality rate by two-thirds, to provide access for all who want reproductive health service and to implement national strategies for sustainable development by 2005 to reverse the loss of environment resources by 2015.

What are the prospects for achieving these goals?

As far as the implementation of the recommendations of

these highly acclaimed international reports is concerned, nothing has been achieved right from the 1950s to the 1990s. International developmental agencies, including that of the UN agencies such as the UNDP and the UNCTAD, have not even been able to scratch the surface. They have indeed often hampered the indigenous efforts of the developing countries. The developing countries remain under the illusion of assistance from these agencies. To make this episode look "authentic", a lot of intellectuals from the Third World, most of them ignorant of the harsh realities of their own countries, do research work in preparing reports on international developmental issues. No less a person than the late French philosopher, Jean-Paul Sartre, said in his "Preface" the widely-known book by the famous Algerian revolutionary and psychiatrist, Frantz Fanon[10], entitled: *The Wretched of the Earth* (1961):

> "The European elite undertook to manufacture native elite. They picked out promising adolescents; they branded them, as with a red-hot iron, with the principles of Western culture; they stuffed their mouths full with high-sounding phrases, grand glutinous words that stuck to the teeth. After a short stay in the mother country they were sent home, whitewashed. These walking lies had nothing left to say to their brothers; they only echoed. From Paris, from London, from Amsterdam we would utter the words "Pantheon Brotherhood", and somewhere in Africa or Asia lips would open ... "Pantheon" ..."Brotherhood". It was the golden age."

There is literally not a single intellectual from the Third World, preparing reports on international developmental issues, who is neither educated in the West nor had some gainful employment in the West on one hand, and who is not Westernized[11] in his outlook, ridiculing his own native culture and civilization.

So the strategies behind not implementing the resolutions adopted at the international forums are very simple: Pick up some leader of international repute from the West[12], let him recommend some "urgent" programmes for cooperation between developed and developing nations. Initiate a few insignificant programmes early in the part of the decade, and do not complete them. Then set up a commission to evaluate the reasons for their "failures" in the middle of the decade. By the time the evaluation is complete the decade is about to finish. So why not start a fresh programme in the new decade?[13] This is the way inaction has been self-perpetuating itself from 1950 till now. We now attempt to analyze this scenario, which is so frustrating and yet keeps on repeating.

Professor Dudley Seers[14], pointed out that the UN International Development Strategy for the 1970s "is dead, like the Pearson Report and the UNCTAD resolutions on which it was based. It has been killed even before its mid-term review scheduled for 1975, by the rise in oil prices from about $ 3 per barrel to $ 11[15] per barrel."

Barbara Ward[16] concluded that "The chief impact of extra costs incurred by the developing nations who do not export oil—a clear $ 15 billion for oil, $ 5½ billion for food and fertilizers, a doubling of prices of other materials and for many manufactured imports and all this in a single year..." This is obvious in one sense, for the economies of the developed nations which have only less than one-third of the total population of the world and control more than 87.5 per cent of the World's GNP, the result is staggering. The pitiable condition of the poor nations' is beyond imagination. Increases on oil price and fertilizers alone have overshadowed the total aid from the rest of the outside world. The UN International Development Strategy for the 1970s, which was formulated for the betterment of the underdeveloped nations, is dead when Barbara Ward stated the dire situation of developed nations, when she even mentioned "the fourth world", implying that the whole world might get engulfed. The Pearson Report, published in 1969, revealed that the fullest development of the world is not possible unless all the people on earth share in the developmental process.

After the Second World War, the 1950s was presumed to be the decade of recovery of the European nations torn by the war. The end of the war also saw the disintegration of the colonial system, the social problems created by the war, to build housing and to rebuild the means of production to provide the consumer goods which were either devastated by the war or converted into the war production. Thus the new States began to emerge by getting rid of the colonial yoke, but this was only 'political freedom', having nothing at their disposal regarding economic independence. This was probably due to the fact that political freedom was granted reluctantly because the liberation movements had grown in their strength and the staggering economies of the colonialists, in the aftermath of the war, could no longer control the colonies.

Later in the 1950s, when Europe had sufficiently recovered from the economic losses sustained in the war, attention was paid for the first time to the former colonies for their economic development in the 1960s. The 1960s thus saw a new era in which the 'aids, loans, and private investments' from the developed nations were initiated. The futility of all these exercises was recognized in their contribution to the development system. The result was growing frustrations and bitterness, expressed by both the developed and the underdeveloped nations. The grief of the underdeveloped nations resulted in the loss of faith and goodwill about the intentions of the developed nations, especially the United States. This bitterness and frustration are well reflected in the Arusha Declaration of President Nyerere[17] of Tanzania.

The Report by the International Commission of International development, whose Chairman was the late Prime Minister of Canada, L.B. Pearson, (published in 1969), clearly indicated that the developed nations had failed to comply on their part in the process of international development. In the beginning of 1970, having realized all these frustrations and the failure of the UNDD-I, fresh efforts were initiated through the United Nations development machinery and new pledges were made for the development. The result was the formulation of the UN International Development Strategy for the 1970s and the launching of the Second UNDD. The lessons of the failures of the 1960s were drawn up, and thus a fresh attempt was made to eliminate hunger and poverty from this troubled world. Now the UN International Development Strategy for the 1970s is dead. It died even before its scheduled mid-term review in 1975. Not a single clause of the Pearson Report had been implemented. None of the UNCTAD I, II, and III, resolutions and agreements had fully implemented. An important question which arises is: of what use is the UN and its specialized agencies which are engaged in the development process[18], when it has no power to implement its resolutions and perform the task it has been given? What does all this indicate? Is it an illusion to keep people in the dark? Is the functionalization of the UN merely to provide international statistics when it is unable to implement its objectives? Is it only for 'scholarly' academic research on paper? Or to provide some positive hope and expectation to those for whom it is formulated: those suffering from hunger, illiteracy, and are unable to protect themselves from the hazards of the climate?

Certainly we cannot be that much pessimistic. There is some, more or less, direct or indirect 'contribution' to the development process, but again the question arises: in what amount? The answer is clear from the fact that the programmes under the UNDP, and the policies formulated in the Development Decades (mentioned earlier) are simply not sufficient enough to have an integrated approach to the economic and social problems of any underdeveloped nation. The development approach has been on a very narrow scale, which is not sufficient enough even to lay down the necessary foundation stone or to provide the required infrastructure for economic and social development.

However, I would like to cite an example on a quantitative basis, "As of mid-1973[19], the UNDP was supporting more than 6,000 projects, valued at $ 3.7 billion, provided international experts, equipments and fellowship, opportunities to help meet basic development need." This means, on calculating, that the number of projects in a country averaged 44.4; thus the total development assistance from this source averages $25.64 million, (of course some countries must be receiving relatively higher amounts and other less). Can we hope to bring about a change in a developing country, or can we provide the necessary infrastructure, with a sum of $26.64 million? Is this not a negligible amount as far as development is concerned? Is this not an illusion in the name of development? No wonder, more than one-half of the developing nations failed even to achieve a 5 per cent annual growth rate in 1972, while the target was set up for 6 per cent. This group[20] alone accounts for almost 40 per cent of the population of the developing world. Egon Glesinger[21] rightly pointed out that we cannot solve development problems by initiating a project here, a project there; here a little irrigation, there a little education, and so on.

However, there is some mistake on the part of the underdeveloped nations themselves. Having emerged from the colonial rule, (an alien functional administration that dominated for centuries) no change in the application and philosophy of the needs and requirements of the people was made. The system of the western nations has been in practice, as it was during the colonial period. External assistance must not be accepted to alienate the country itself from its socio-cultural value systems under the phony virtue of economic development. Thus political integration should not only link with economic integration but also with social factors. The establishment of any economic and political practice must be appropriate to the particular situation in time.

External assistance and international cooperation is now recognized by the undeveloped nations as an illusion. The designation of these Development Decades, as the sheet of facts and opinion prepared by the Vienna Institute[22], outlined in the first paragraph, reads: "The designation of the 1960s as the UNDD has created on public opinion the wrong impression that a break-through could be achieved within a period of only ten years." The achievements and accomplishments of the 1st UNDD and the mid-term review of the 2nd UNDD, made officially available in 1975 showed no break-through, as far as development is concerned.

All this led to the conclusion that development could only

be made possible through self-help, though this is a slower process. The Arusha[23] Declaration is an example.

Though I have been so far criticizing the role of foreign factors in the development process, my view is to coordinate the available material resources, the capital, and the manpower from either source.

It is the prior decision-making that carries in it the mechanics of guaranteed failure. This is the reason behind the failures of the international conferences. At the end, the outcome of the whole conference usually turns out to be an illusion. Why a international illusion? Because the final output results is three things at the end of the conferences:

1. Impractical resolutions are, in many cases, accepted by the underdeveloped nations reluctantly, because they have no other choice;
2. The agreement to disagree and to arrange another conference may be up to four years—the UNCTAD, for example. This, too, drags the issues out, and sweeps the urgent and bare necessities of more than two-thirds of the people on earth under the political rug;
3. The collection of the fresh statistics of the nations; how much poorer nations have become, and how much more the rich nations have accumulated, thus ensuring that the economic gap goes on increasing.

Thus the deliberations of the conference turn out to be like going to a circus or watching a theatre.

At the end of the 1st UNDD and at the beginning of the 2nd UNDD, be frustrated at the outcome and accomplishment of the 1st UNDD, the government of Upper Volta[24] declared that it couldn't participate in a second attempt to hoax the people. The government of Chile commented that the 'lack of political will to implement the strategy is one of the many illusions and tricks with which the developed countries have deluded the poor countries for many years. My government does not want to be associated with a new illusion and a new trick'. The analysis of the words, "new illusion" and "new trick", indicate lack of faith in the 2nd UNDD. At the Algiers

Conference of the Non-aligned nations in September 1973, Prime Minister Indira Gandhi[25], said,

> "When we became free, it was with high hopes of bringing about immediate changes in our society. We thought the process of transformation, once initiated and pursued with fervour, would get momentum. But political and economic interests, domestic as well as international, have proved formidable obstructions. As the economic struggle becomes more acute, the long suppressed voices of the people sharpen; but with every step forward, the resistance of entrenched groups, often aligned with foreign interests, especially the faceless multi-national corporations, become vehement, unscrupulous, and at the same time, more subtle and even insidious, for it is no longer overt but indirectly subversive and provocative. In India, we see these constraints everyday."

This statement clearly indicates the feeling of exploitation. This is exactly what I concluded in Chapter 7 about total payments of amortization and interests. The amount of total capital outflow in the form of repatriated profits, service payments, interests and the amortization exceeds the total investment and aid and we reach an unorthodox situation where a decision has to be made to 'gain' 'profits' 'from losses' of 'aid'.

Another example of such cooperation through conferences and their illusions, is the Yaunde Talks[26] between the nine nations of EEC and almost fifty developing countries, where McLean and Maxwell argued, "that the talks are a waste of breath, that they have built into them the mechanics of guaranteed failure, that all the major decisions have already been taken, and that there is now a need for a completely new strategy for the poor world nations and their supporters in Europe."

It is obvious that there is a lack of goodwill on the part of the developed world, and that it just wants the poor world to remain its parasite while pretending to attempt self-reliance. This is exactly what Lester Pearson[27] concluded regarding aid:

"And since aid, is in some measure simply a way of keeping the poorer community in a position of dependence on the aid-giver, this too, perpetuates, what is in essence a colonial relationship." Dr. Martin Luther King[28], Jr. said:

> "We in the West must bear in mind that the poor countries are poor primarily because we have exploited them through political or economic colonialism."

He mentioned certain stages of development, starting from the traditional way of life and leading eventually towards the high dynamics of development (self-reliance being the object) and pointed out that some of these stages of development might be skipped or be accelerated through international cooperation and global partnership, in other words, on humanitarian grounds, or the way it has been recommended in the Pearson report, *Partners in Development*. The recommendations made in the Jackson's Capacity Study of the UN Development System can further supplement the idea and promote implementations of the resolutions and agreements reached after the lengthy, and expensive international conferences (e.g. GATT, UNCTAD, FAO, to be to name few). These have also turned out to be an illusion.

Through unconditional international cooperation, goodwill, and mutual understanding among the nations within the framework of the UN Charter and its various specialized agencies, we can achieve our common goal: peace and development of the underdeveloped, if we clearly define our subject and object. The subject is food, shelter, clothing, and literacy; the object is to achieve these goals. Development and modernization is, above all for humanity itself, and has to be worked out by the people themselves.

The question now arises: why there should be an international strategy and a global partnership for these underdeveloped nations? Why should the developed nations care about the poverty of these underdeveloped nations? They are alone responsible for their poverty and hunger. Before I discuss this, I would like to mention two opposing views: Prof. P.T. Bauer[29] holds that, if you can help yourself, you can't really be helped from outside; Prof. Rene Dumont replies that, if you could help yourself, you wouldn't need aid. However, it is certain that development will emerge from within the individual nation's economic infrastructure, based on self-reliance as much as possible. The post-war economic aid to European nations under the so called Marshall Plan, and from the Soviet Union as well, and the aid and assistance the underdeveloped nations of today have to be looked at in different perspectives. The former was to restore stability, which was wrecked because of the war. At the same time, though war weary and torn, European nations had the seeds of development in their soil. While in the latter case, the underdeveloped nations of today have to develop from the beginning, for these nations are emerging from the ruthless colonial oppression[30] and suppression, which had no justice whatsoever. Before the post-war period, during the 17th, 18th and 19th centuries, when Europe was developing through industrialization, the underdeveloped nations of today were colonies exploited by their respective rulers, and were thus kept away the line of development. Prof. Bauer's conclusion[31] that *"if you (underdeveloped nations) can't help yourself, you can't really be helped from outside,"* and "that Europe developed without aid," is not really acceptable. As a matter of fact, Europe did not develop without aid, but developed with the sweat and blood and almost unpaid manpower and on the natural resources of the colonies for which not a single penny was paid in commercial return. An embarrassing fact is that it was the Britain of Prof. Bauer, the number one among all the European nations which was engaged in this 'bonanza' and which Prof. Bauer has completely ignored.

We should look into all these historical aspects of the 'bonanza' during the colonial time and consider the suggestions mentioned in the Pearson Report[32].

In formulating the international strategy for development, the negative socio-cultural aspects must be taken into serious consideration, and every attempt must be made to avoid them or at the least minimize them to reduce the negative effect on the system. It must be acknowledged that, although there has been constant rise and development of non-alignment and socialism, the disintegration of the colonial system has given political freedom to former colonies, but as far as economic freedom is concerned, the existing interdependence of the free market economies is going in a direction against these non-aligned sovereign nations and the gap is ever-increasing between the rich and the poor nations. This can only by narrowed through voluntary participation of the developed nations. This will create and promote an environment that would eventually avoid the formation of regional economic interdependent blocks, which we see today between the developed, and the developing nations.

Since the major concern of the UN is being focused towards making an attempt to collaborate between nations to end the poverty of nations, it has now become immediately important to keep in mind that the loss of faith and trust on the part of the underdeveloped nations, arising as a result of their continued exploitation and plunder in the name of aid and loans as discussed in Chapter 7, while formulating any strategy for development. It is now essential and should be the part of the policy planning of the developed nations to transform this 'Divide and Rule Economically' policy into "Unite and Rule by themselves" policy. Of course during the çolonial rule the policy was 'Divide and Rule Directly'. The change in the attitude of the developed nations is much more important and will be much more of a contribution to the poor nations in their just struggle for economic independence. To reduce this loss of faith is now very urgent, otherwise the consequences might be serious in terms of international peace and security.

Probably, Barbara Ward[33] realized these consequences when she wrote, "Critics do not try to find out inconsiderable evidence of success because they have lost interest in the policy. Nor do they accept inevitable errors, as they would, say, in defence, because particular mistakes are acceptable only when general policy is supported. It is this overall acceptance of aid that is weakening." Any form of oppression will not allow the poor nations to stand on their own feet. The attainment of self-reliance through international cooperation is a remote desire, unless a *"go it alone"* policy is adopted. Change in ideology cannot be made overnight, for change is a slow and gradual process.

The economic interdependence of the free market economies should not endanger the sovereignty of the poor nations, and it need not necessarily be an intervention in the internal affairs of the nations. With this, the resources of this planet can be prevented from being consumed by destructive and weary wars. A closer co-operation of the economies of the nations and their interdependence based upon mutual respect and sharing of appropriate benefits, will stimulate and accelerate the international development process. The economic development of the underdeveloped nations[34], as far as the role of external factors is concerned, should be directed towards setting up of new means as well as providing favourable export markets for their products. In this respect, the contribution of the developed socialist countries, led by the USSR, have been far greater than the Western capital States, led by the USA.

The underdeveloped nations have little access to the Western capital markets, and in addition they have to import food, fuel, chemicals and fertilizers. Efforts now should be directed towards global development to combat hunger and poverty. The peoples of the three continents of Africa, Asia and the Latin America do not want war. They want better living conditions, jobs, good housing, food, clothing and education—the bare necessities of life needed to live like human beings and to realize what human dignity means. Unfortunately they have enough wars thrust upon them, largely to serve the interests of some 'super power'.[35] Who was fighting in Korea—the Koreans or the materials supplied by the 'super powers'? Who was fighting in Vietnam—the Vietnamese or the material supplied by the 'super powers'. Who has been fighting in the Indian subcontinent—the starving masses or the material supplied by the 'super powers'? Who has been fighting in the Middle East—Arabs and Israelis or the material supplied by the 'super powers'. If the 'super powers' do not supply the arms to the hungry people of the underdeveloped nations, there is no way that these poor nations can afford to fight or even can think of fighting and waging wars, let alone actually go on to war.

The former Secretary-General of the United Nations[36], U Thant said in 1969, that "if such a global partnership is not forged within the next decade, then I very much fear that the problems I have mentioned will have reached such staggering proportions that they will be beyond our capacity to control." From this statement, it is clear that, regardless of the dimensions of the problems fasting the mankind, regardless of the grave situations that have been reached, we still have time left to make joint efforts, whatever be social value systems, whatever our 'ism', the socialism, the capitalism, the non-alignment, or the 'ism' of Mao tse-Tung, which cut off the relation with the rest of the world in the 1950s and 1960s. The problem of underdevelopment is the common problem of all the 'isms' and can well be fought together for the benefit of all. That would be the real solution to the problem of poverty.

The strategy behind aid and assistance should enable the recipient to achieve the needed self-reliance and not to make him a parasite or a permanent dependent. The latter aspect gives term "aid" the meaning "imperialism" or exploitation of the recipient nation. The recipient underdeveloped nation is expected to show enthusiasm and the developed nation (donor nation) should be expected to guide the poor nation to develop and not to misguide and exploit her in the name of advice and assistance. The objective evaluation of such strategies will be in the interest of all humanity and in maintaining peace and security for all the inhabitants on earth.

A factor that is missing between the donor and the recipient nation is the proper understanding of each other's position, problems, and social value systems at home. The donor nations usually keep reservations regarding development of the recipient along her (donor) own lines; while the interests of the recipient nation are best served if the lines are drawn in accordance with the frame of her own social and cultural value systems, her functional social theories and practice. This will instill a trust and faith in the intentions of the donor nation, which will mean increased friendship.

The three main policy generating 'isms' are liberalism, conservatism, and the so called radicalism. The development strategy of the poor nation has to be worked out in close coordination of all these three 'isms'. Being liberal alone poses problems in the implementation of the policies; being conservative alone and following the traditional way can no longer be accepted if we have to keep pace with the technological renovations of today; and being radical may well create more problems than it could resolve. But we need radical policy recommendations to bring about the change, to break the stagnation, and to make the social systems dynamic. The policy generating machinery, so formulated, will produce the forces that will inevitably accelerate the development system.

In making such policy recommendations, it is pertinent to mention the present trend in trade between the developed and the underdeveloped nations which, in the words of Lester Pearson[37], former Canadian Prime Minister, is that the "trade and investment carried on between unequal partners do not produce sustained growth for the weaker party. From the crippling state of subjection, the only escape is the clean-break; the kind of break thc Japanese imposed on Western traders and missionaries in 17th century—a stronger version, if you like, of America's revolutionary break with the British trading system in 1776, a break comparative to that of Russia turning inwards in 1928 and launching the First Five-Year Plan."

In the Arusha Declaration[38], Tanzania formulates the policy, makes a plan to have a seriously look at 'aid' and 'co-operation', and emphasizes her traditional way of agriculture and other optimal utilization of whatever scarce resources are available[39]. The questions now arise whether the clear-break is the only solution left for the underdeveloped nations today? Is there no place for humanitarian grounds and unconditional international cooperation? Do these poor nations have to go through bitterness, formulating the strategies, which could otherwise be avoided? I think in formulating the strategies, we have to re-define our existing terminology of 'aid' and 'investment'. The Netherlands Minister for aid to developing countries, B.J. Udink[40], prefers 'co-operation' to 'assistance'. We must take care not to divide the world into two categories: those who receive assistance and those who give it. In fact, we are all involved. We are all passengers in the same boat of international co-operation.

When the United States emerged, its first President, George Washington, held that the US was being exploited by British merchants and hampered by British regulations. This eventually led President James Madison[41] on June 1, 1812 to declare war on the British. The British ignored all these frustrations felt by the United States, managed to enter Washington DC, and set fire to the White House and the Capitol.

In light of these historical facts, the United States, one of the mightiest nations in the world, now needs to change her ideology about the underdeveloped nations. The poor nations feel exactly the same way about the United States as the US felt about Britain, and which eventually led to war.

Victor Hugo[42] said that "the guilty one is not he who commits the sin, but he who causes the darkness." From the middle of the 19th century, when the industrial revolution was in full swing in Europe and North America, today's underdeveloped nations were under their colonial yoke and were deliberately kept off the line of development. The words of Victor Hugo mean that the former colonialists are the "sinner and thus responsible for the poverty of the poor nations." It is amazing to note that these "sinners" even brand the poor nations as 'backwards', without realizing the darkness they caused. It is thus imperative, on moral and humanitarian grounds, for the developed nations to come forward to help these nations to get rid of poverty and misery.

The responsibility for peace and international security lies on all the nations around the globe. The UN rostrum provides the necessary forum for global partnership. The only thing needed is goodwill and the realization of the responsibility. With change in the ideology of the developed nations, the 'developing' nations will in a real sense be developing. Of course today, we cannot use the term "developing", because the poor nations are not developing at all. This is evident from the fact that the economic gap between the rich and the poor nations is increasing and the ratio of the imports to NDP is not lowering, which are imperatives for avoiding deficit in balance of payments.

The change in the attitude and ideology of the developed nations, together with the blowing winds of detente with the Soviets and other developed Eastern European nations may lead to the path of peace, progress, and prosperity for all mankind and may eliminate the fear and insecurity towards each other that now exist between the nations.

Thus with this discussion I can conclude that, for development, global partnership is necessary in the implementation of the strategies.

From the previous Chapters 2 and 3, based largely on quantitative discussion, it is evident that the aids, loans and development assistance have not been able to contribute significantly to the development process. The Pearson report has a number of recommendations and almost none has been implemented since its publication in 1969. So is the case with UNCTAD I, II and III resolutions. Similar things were realized at a DAC member nations meeting in Tokyo in September 1970. They did stress the easing and untying of aids, but nothing has really been carried out.

The aid and investments from the free market economies and the centrally planned economies have two distinct characteristics. Free market economies provide manufactured goods and interest-bearing loans and tied aid and grants, the repayments of which hinder nations authentic development. From centrally planned economies, the developed socialist countries, assistance is concentrated largely on industrial development, setting up of manufacturing plants, and relatively low interest-bearing loans. In this sense, the assistance from centrally planned economies have two distinct advantages over the assistance from free market economies (i) low interest rate, usually for a longer period, eases the burden of the repayment of interest and amortization, and (ii) the underdeveloped nation receives means of production. This provides the sound basis for necessary infrastructure.

The failure of the UNCTAD 68 New Delhi was inevitable. This is because the US made a proposal[43] "nor would we grant preferences to low developed countries that gave exclusive trade preferences to any developed country." As a matter of fact if this proposal is not to make the underdeveloped nations suffer, it is certainly does not help them to grow. This is against, in its totality, what their late President J.F. Kennedy[44] hoped of the American foreign aid, "for a better life based on economic progress, education, social justice and the development of stable institutions...our military and economic programmes aid to seek". And further, so long as the objectives and criteria for foreign assistance is[45], "to allocate a given sum among a number of countries so as to produce a pattern of social development that is in the best interest of the United States," there will never be development or acceleration in development. This means that[46] the situation will become even worse in the future years. If the amount of new loans increases at the same rhythm as in 1965-67, by 1977 the cost of servicing the foreign public debt alone rose to US $ 9.2 thousand million as against $5.2 thousand million in 1969. If we add the revenues (profits and interests) realized on private investments, which in 1977 reached $8 thousand million of the minimum, the outflow of capital exceeded the total amount of capital receipts coming from abroad. Hence we arrive at the paradox *"Who aids whom"?* [*Stated in Chapter* 2(C)]. Seeing this trend of development, Lester B. Pearson[47] said, while answering the statements made at the Columbia University Conference on International Development, held in February 1970, in New York, that *"on the whole the evidence suggests that economic assistance has, at best, made little contribution to the aided nations' growth and at most, has seriously distorted it."*

Now let us look at some other alternatives to make the development assistance from the international development agencies more effective. It should be designed in a way so as to be beneficial to both the donor and the recipient. One of the main reasons for the amount of money that is being repatriated to the donor nations is that this money simply could not be reinvested in the poor nations because of lack of business. Now the developed nations can help establish small-scale industries that do not need much sophisticated technology, so that the poor nations can reinvest the repatriated money. After this, the developed nations should trade and import some manufactured goods from those poor countries. This would be beneficial to both groups, the developed and the underdeveloped, in a number of ways:

1. The reinvestment of what is repatriated today would help the developing nations in their struggle for economic independence. It would help move the take off process towards self-sustained growth faster. It would help them in industrialization and urbanization, without much suffering from scarcity of foreign exchange.
2. The scarcity of foreign exchange is, more or less, being financed by the developed nations in the form of loans and grants. With reinvestment, the aids and grants would soon no longer be needed.
3. Reinvestment would reduce the foreign borrowings, which cause the danger that new loans could dry up and foreign exchange earnings fall.
4. The economic development of the underdeveloped, in this way, is in the long-term interests of the developed nations. It generates trade.
5. At the same time, the developing nations themselves have to provide the political stability to encourage investment and keep the tax rate at a lower level.

Hence in India and in any other country in South Asia, economic reforms are being carried out since 1991 have not been able to bear fruit at all, as far as the lot of the teeming millions suffering from poverty is concerned. Kristoffel Lieten[48] stated that:

> "It has been argued that India had a restrictive, inward-looking regime, and that, therefore, the economic breakthrough could not come about. Beginning around 1980 with the first IMF, and speeded up with the radical changes in economic policy around 1990, India opted for an export-led and foreign-capital-driven development. The fruits of such development should have become visible, but they have not. The Indian upper middle classes have gained access to cable television, cellular phones, computers and king-size cigarettes. The goods remain by and large restricted to a one-digit percentage of the population. The vast majority of the population has hardly seen progress. GNP growth patterns have remained at the levels of the 1960s and 1970s, occasionally going up, as they did over the last two decades, attracting eulogies for the policy of liberalization, and then falling again, as they had done in the past. While on the one hand growth has not picked up, on the other hand, the government has lost much of its power to direct investments into development-promoting and socially necessary product lines. It has also lost much of the power to check regional imbalances and to fight poverty."

Aids, loans and grants at this time are not proving effective, but in the way mentioned above, they could be a great contribution to both the developed and the underdeveloped. There would then emerge real peace and prosperity for all nations, without a burden being placed on any rich nation to provide 'aid'. Gunnar Myrdal says truly that trade, and not aid, will be the real test of our development. Along with this, improved trade helps enrich social, political, and cultural environment.

Now that the cold war has ended between the USA and the erstwhile USSR (with the disintegration of the latter), we certainly have what the three statesmen of international repute wished for the welfare of the plight of the peoples in the Third World, Messrs Ingvar Carlsson, Julius Nyerere and Willy Brandt, in their joint communication in May 1991[49] :

> "The transformation of relations between East and West has ended the Cold War. Freeing minds and resources that for so long were bound by sterile confrontation. ...
>
> We have an historical opportunity to change the way we deal with the world's increasing interdependencies."

The cold war thus has ended between erstwhile USSR and Communist Block on the one hand, and North America and Western Europe on the other. Similar efforts are indeed appreciable in South Asia under SAARC, as initiated by eminent citizens of the region under the chairmanship of the former Prime Minister of India Shri I.K. Gujral[50]:

> We have before us the experience of detente between the East and the West and the confidence-building measures undertaken by two sides of divided Europe through the Helsinki process that finally led to the end of the Cold War, the establishment of the Organization for Security and Cooperation in Europe (OSCE). The Europeans were able to overcome the animosities created through two world wars and centuries of intra-European wars.
>
> Eminent personalities from India, Bangladesh, Bhutan, Maldives, Nepal, Pakistan and Sri Lanka have formed a citizens' commission for South Asia and brought out a joint declaration after their first meeting in Kathmandu on December 1-3, 2000. The chairperson of the group is former Prime Minister Inder Kumar Gujral and includes personalities with both stature and credibility not only in their respective countries but also in the world outside. The objective of the commission is a very laudable one, to stress the major role and responsibility of civil society in creating a favourable opinion for promotion of regional cooperation. It has urged the governments, opinion-makers and civil society of the SAARC member countries to reaffirm their political will to work collectively for peace, progress and prosperity with a view to improving the quality of life of one-fifth of humankind.

## NOTES

1. *The Hindustan Times*, New Delhi, 16-5-1991, p.13. Ingvar Carlsson is Prime Minister of Sweden since 1986, Julius Nyerere, Africa's elder statesman, was Tanzania's first President, a post he held from 1962-1985. Willy Brandt was Chancellor of West Germany from 1969-1974 and won the Nobel Peace Prize in 1971.
2. UNDD-I or the United Nations Development Decade-I was launched by the United Nations in 1950.
3. UNDD-II or the United Nations Development Decade-II, was launched by the United Nations in 1960.
4. Partners in Development, (New York: Praeger Pub., 1969), a report on development issues in the Third World in collaboration with the Western powers, was prepared by a panel of experts selected from around the world, under the Chairmanship of L.B. Pearson, former Canadian Prime Minister and a Nobel Laureate for Peace. This report was commissioned by the World Bank [or International Bank for Reconstruction and Development (IBRD)].
5. *North-South: A Programme for Survival*, (Cambridge, Mass,: The M.I.T. Press, 1980). This is a report on development issues with rather compassionate appeal, prepared under the chairmanship of Willy Brandt, former Chancellor of West Germany, and also a Nobel Laureate for Peace. Brandt was Chairman of the Independent Commission on International Development Issues.
6. *Ibid.*, p. 290.
7. *The Challenge to the South*: The Report of the South Commission, (New York: Oxford University Press, 1990), pp. 226-28. This Report was prepared by the South Commission under the chairmanship of the former president of Tanzania, Julius K. Nyerere. India's Dr. Man Mohan Singh, former Governor of the Reserve Bank of India, and now Minister of Finance since 1991, is one of the principal author of this Report.
8. *Ibid.*, pp. 226-28.
9. *Human Development Report 2001*, UNDP, Oxford University Press, New York, 2001, pp. 21, 24.
10. Frantz Fanon, *The Wretched of Earth*, (New York: The Grove Press, 1968). This book was originally published in French in France, in 1961.
11. It is not uncommon for professors in Western Universities, especially North American ones, to brand any student for the Third World "ideal" or "aggressive", "not pragmatic", etc. who dares question the wisdom of Westernization of his native land. If that student continues to persist in his beliefs, these professors, the reactionary intellectuals, then do not hesitate to remark..." you honestly worked

hard, but your analysis is not very critical, and it does not really meet the academic standards of this professional "Graduate School," giving him a failing grade and throw him out.

12. L.B. Pearson, who retired from active politics, was Prime Minister of Canada, who chaired the Commission on Development for the 1970's. See Partners in Development, footnote 3 above. Mr. W. Brandt was former chancellor of West Germany, who chaired the Commission on Development for the 1980s. *See North-South: A Programme for Survival,* footnote 4 above.
13. It is quite clear from the series as outlined in footnotes 2, 3, 4, 5 and 7. They are:
    (a) For the 1950s: The UNDD-I
    (b) For the 1960s: the UNDD-II
    (c) For the 1970s: The Pearson Report, titled *Partners in Development*
    (d) For the 1980s: The Brandt Commission report titled *North-South*
    (e) For the 1990s: *The Challenge to the South*: The South Commission Report
    (f) For the 2000s, the Millennium's first decade, *United Nations Millennium Declaration.*
14. In *Development Forum,* a U.N. monthly newspaper, March, 1974.
15. The price of oil, in fact, continued to escalate, and reached close to $ 40.00 a barrel. However, since Ronald Reagan tookover the presidency of the United States of America in January 1980, the recession began to set in the Western World. With it, recently, the price of oil has begun to slash down, but is still in the $ 30 a barrel range.
16. Barbara Ward, "World First, Second, Third and Fourth", in *Economist Magazine,* London, England, May 19, 1974, p. 65.
17. The Arusha Declaration marked a turning point in Tanzanian politics. For the text of this Declaration, see Julius K. Nyerere, Freedom and Socialism, (Dar-es-Salaam: Oxford University Press, 1968), pp.231-50.
18. In mid-1970s, about 80 per cent of the U.N. budget and 90 per cent of its manpower were being spent only on development efforts.
19. United Nations Development Programme. The Administrator's Report, United Nations, New York, 1973, p. 2.
20. *Ibid.,* p. 4.
21. In Colin Legun (ed.), The Ist U.N. Development Decade (UNDD) and its lessons for the 1970s, (New York: Praeger Pub., 1970), p. 39.
22. Amlan Data, in Colin Legun, *op. cit.,* p. 49.
23. For Arusha declaration, see footnote 17.
24. New Internationalist, monthly magazine, Devon Press, Berkshire, England, January, 1974, p. 1.

25. Quoted by S.G. Sardesai, "Achievements and Difficulties of Non-Alignment", in World Marxist Review, Toronto, March 1974; p. 80.
26. McLean and Maxwell, "Press Berlin to Brusells" in New Internationalist Devon Press, Berkshire, England, January 1974, p. 12.
27. L.B. Pearson, "Pearson on Pearson Report", in CERES magazine, FAO of the United Nations, Rome, Italy, March-April, 1970, p. 26.
28. Martin Luther King, Jr., *Conscience for Change*, (Toronto: Canadian Broadcasting Corporation, 1967), p. 36.
29. See "P.T. Bauer vs. Rene Dumont; Debate on Aid", in *CERES Magazine*, FAO of the United Nations, Rome, Italy, January-February, 1970, p. 33.
30. The end to colonial era began in the aftermath of the Second World War, 1939-45, when the colonialists, e.g. English and French, simply could not control the colonies thousands of miles away, India was the first to be freed in 1947. Much of Africa was freed in the 1960s, Rhodesia, now called Zimbabwe, was freed in 1979. South Africa also finally got her Black population majority rule in 1990.
31. "P.T. Bauer Vs. Rene Dumont: Debate on Aid", *op. cit.*, pp. 31-41.
32. *Partners in Development*, (New York: Praeger Pub., 1969), a report on development issues in the Third World in collaboration with the Western powers, was prepared by a panel of experts selected from around the world, under the Chairmanship of L.B. Pearson.
33. Barbara Ward, "Action for the Future," in D. Mumby, (ed.), *World Development*, (Washington DC: Corpus Books, 1969), p. 176.
34. *See* statement made by Indira Gandhi in footnote 25.
35. With the disintegration of the erstwhile USSR in 1990 and the subsequent pledge of the president of Russia, (the largest of the republic of the former USSR, now called the CIS, the Commonwealth of the Independent States), there is the hope that the cold war would end soon and that the former super powers would have meaningful and constructive approach towards global peace and security, as pledged by the presidents of the USA and Russia.
36. Robert Theobald, *The Challenge of a Decade*, (New York: United Nations, 1971), title page.
37. L.B. Pearson, "Pearson on Pearson Report", in *CERES Magazine*, FAO of the United Nations, Rome, Italy, March-April, 1970, p. 24.
38. *See* under footnote 17.
39. Sures Chandra Jain, *The Indigenous Resources for Rural Development: Agricultural Mechanization and Rural Industrialization*, Concept Publishing Co., New Delhi, 2004.
40. B.J. Udink, in *CERES Magazine*, FAO of the United Nations, Rome, Italy, Jan.-Feb., 1969, p. 28.

41. The Presidents of the USA, White House Historical Association, Washington DC, 1973, p. 15.
42. Quoted by Martin Luther King, Jr., *Conscience for Change*, (Toronto: Canadian Broadcasting Corporation, 1967), p. 4.
43. W.L. Thorp, *The Reality of Foreign Aid*, (New York: Praeger Pub., 1971), p. 283.
44. John F. Kannedy, "Foreign Aid", in R.A. Goldwin, (ed.), Why Foreign Aid, (Chicago: Rand Menally, 1963), p. 133.
45. H.B. Chenery, "Objectives and Criteria for Foreign Assistance", in R.A. Goldwin, (ed.), *Ibid.*, p. 37.
46. Angelo Angelopolous, "Who Aids Whom", in R.A. Goldwin, (ed.), *Why Foreign Aid*, (Chicago: Rand Menally, 1963), p. 133.
47. Lester B. Pearson, "Pearson on Pearson Report," in *CERES Magazine*, FAO of the United Nations, Rome, Italy, March-April, 1970, p. 20.
48. Kristoffel Lieten, Multinationals and Development: Revisiting the Debate, in Frans J. Schuurman, Ed., *Globalization and Development Studies: Challenges for the 21st Century*, Vistaar Publications (A division of Sage Pub.), New Delhi, 2001, p. 112.
49. *The Hindustan Times*, New Delhi, 16-5-1991, p. 13.
50. K. Subrahmanyam, A Citizens' Commission: Strengthen Civil Society in South Asia, *Times of India*, New Delhi, 18-12-2000, p. 12.

# 5

# Globalization and Economic Reforms for Perpetuating Poverty

*"(In the aftermath of the failure of communism in the former USSR and Eastern Europe), it is not a matter of shame but of a tragedy that we are now switching to Western capitalism from the Russian socialism. Just as the Russian socialist model was not capable to solve our problems in India, similarly the free market capitalist system of the West will also not be able to solve our problems.*

*Who other than Mahatma Gandhi in this country understood that solution to a problem emerges only from the point from where the problem originates. Nothing can be achieved with borrowed keys. There is no way in India other than the Gandhian way."*

—*Prabhat Joshi*[1], *1991*

*"...That if there ever was anything like globalization then that is already over because we have now entered a period of increasing fragmentation and de-globalization."*

—*Frans J. Schuurman*[2], *2001*

*"Beginning around 1980 with the first IMF, and speeded up with the radical changes in economic policy around 1990, India opted for an export-led and foreign-capital-driven development. The fruits of such development should have become visible, but they have not."*

—*Kristoffel Lieten*[3], *2001*

External aid and loan can become a catalyst in the development projects, if conditions are favourable to the underdeveloped nations.

In various chapters in this Book, the picture so far and the future prospects indicate conflict, non-cooperation, a gloomy outlook, and frustrated desires on the part of the underdeveloped nations, precisely because the developed countries have not been fair enough to analyze all the problems facing the poor countries. In spite of this gloomy picture, however, man for man creates the problems. Let us now be optimistic. I cannot see any reason why we cannot transform all these gloomy and frustrating outcomes into a positive contribution to help fight hunger, illiteracy and provide shelter and clothing to more than two-thirds of the people on earth over the three continents of Africa, Asia and Latin America. The fulfilling of these basic necessities and requirements will help create a feeling of dignity and responsibility among these masses. This will eventually enable them to help themselves, in other words, to be self-reliant. The lawlessness, social disorders, and unequal opportunities are the phenomena that set the stages for change, change in the existing socio-cultural value system. With the necessity of social change, an idea of revolution is inevitable. Revolution and brütality especially the suppression of human freedom are almost synonymous. But a planned revolution does not necessarily have to be brutal and barbaric to bring about a social change and to create the required momentum necessary for it. This change, in terms of international development, can only be made through goodwill and unconditional international cooperation, based upon mutual respect and peaceful coexistence among the nation involved within the existing UN system. In other words, it will mean influencing the national goals with broad international planning.

Professor Jozsef Bognar said that it could perform three fundamental services[4]:

1. Promote endeavours of a humanitarian nature, such as the prevention of famine, hunger and under-nourishment;
2. Promote and coordinate national plans, and regional and continental economic integrations;

3. Encourage the rationalization of the international division of labour.

In November 1997 the Institute of Development Studies of the University of Nijmegen in the Netherlands organized a workshop on the significance of globalization (as a concept, a theory, a discourse and/or as an ontological process) for development studies in developing countries. The following summary of the views of the many scholars who presented their papers in this workshop[5]:

Reinhart Kossler[6]: "Globalization may be considered a complex and multi-dimensional set of processes of rapid change, while at the same time delineating a programme of fundamental and multi-dimensional change and an ideology to legitimize such change."

Frans J. Schuurman[7]: "...That if there ever was anything like globalization then that is already over because we have now entered a period of increasing fragmentation and de-globalization."

Kristoffel Lieten[8]: "Globalization and destabilization are coinciding phenomena; a causal relationship is probable."

Reinhart Kossler[9]: "In a time of enhanced globalization, inequality of life chances and life levels on a world scale has become an ever more acute problem."

Ton van Naerssen[10]: "Global cities are not only sites for the accumulation of capital but also major sites for the creation of a new global culture. It is in these cities, and particularly in the world cities, that new cultural and political identities are being constructed."

Frans J. Schuurman[11]: "...Globalization is...primarily cultural in nature. ...Traditional identities are under threat indigenous people are alienated from their cultural heritage through the global movement of consumer capitalism."

Kristoffel Lieten[12]: "Beginning around 1980 with the first IMF, and speeded up with the radical changes in economic policy around 1990, India opted for an export-led and foreign-capital-driven develop-ment. The fruits of such development should have become visible, but they have not."

What do the above noted views of so many scholars mean about the outcome of the globalization and economic reforms? All this indicates that we need a new thinking, new ideas to resolve the crisis and conflicts. This is imperative when the role of external factors in development and modernization has reached a critical situation, such that the underdeveloped nations have begun to think, *"Who aids whom"* and calculate 'profits' from 'losses' of 'aid' and 'investment'. In such a state, neither side can be really blamed, developed or under-developed. We have to find the reasons and causes behind such motivations to seek out the truth. The reason and the truth is simple enough. Why should the rich nations give out their wealth and why should they not make profits on their investments? The poor nations suffer, especially when these masses of the three continents no more ignorant of their poverty when they have seen some of their fellows enjoying the 'luxuries' of TV, Radio, Telephones, Cars, etc. We have to resolve this crisis:

1. From the donor nations' point of view we want to aid and invest but business is business and it means making profits;
2. From the poor nations' point of view; we want to be aided and welcome investment, but the capital outflow can no longer be allowed to exceed the total capital inflow.

The analytical review of these two situations reveals, as

I said earlier, that both are justified in their relative positions. (i) One must make profits but they should not exceed the total inflow for three reasons, (ii) the underdeveloped nations will then be facing the balance of payments problem, (iii) it will be difficult to control inflation, and finally, (iv) the ratio of imports to NDP will go higher. It is necessary that the capital outflow in the form of interests, profits repatriated, and service payments should not exceed the total capital inflow into the underdeveloped nation, otherwise what is the contribution of foreign aid and loans in the role of development? I would like to mention "a four-point prescription" to resolve this conflict between the foreign interests and those of the Third World countries, as pointed out by Professor Paul Streeten[13]:

1. To reduce the political tensions that arise from the large foreign-owned enclaves in less developed countries and fears of expropriations, which deter foreign enterprise.
2. To establish a framework which would change the policies of the foreign companies so that they do not necessarily subordinate the policies of the local companies to the interests of the parent companies?
3. To induce spread effects, so that the beneficial activities of the foreign companies spill over into the less dynamic sectors of the rest of the economy.
4. To set free, after a period, the scarce foreign capital and skills so that these can be re-employed in existing activities.

Prescription number one considers the fear of expropriations which deters foreign enterprise, and only arises when the foreign enterprises get involved in the domestic affairs of the host country and begin to influence the host government in her policy-planning to suit their own selfish ends. This is exactly what Mrs. Indira Gandhi[14] said in September 1973 at the Algiers Conference of the non-aligned nations, "...With every step forward, the resistance of the entrenched groups, often aligned with foreign interests, especially the faceless multinational corporations, becomes more vehement." 'Prescription' number two to four are essentially what has been formulated in the Pearson Report[15], that there is a lack of goodwill and cooperation on the part of the developed nations and that the fullest development and exploration of this planet is not possible until and unless all humanity on the earth share together and joint venture is undertaken. This is what Professor Hans Singer[16] said "about the crisis in the poorer countries, which will be world crisis—let there be no doubt that this can be avoided by the enlightened policies." Sweden has abolished tied aid by law. Part of the Canadian aid, about 20 per cent is untied, as are the generous policies of the Netherlands, Switzerland, and other Scandinavian nations.

What is the Arusha Declaration[17]? It merely reflects the feeling of frustration and exploitation as far as the role of foreign aid and loans in development is concerned. President Nyerere, then in Arusha Declaration[18], formulated the policy of self-reliance and socialism based upon the theme that "a poor man does not use the money as a weapon." Dangers of depending upon foreign aid were well realized, in spite of the fact that inflow of foreign capital increases the resources available in the country and helps to import the necessary machinery and technical know-how as well. But when capital outflow exceeds the inflow, then it becomes a negative effect on the development system. This situation can no longer be accepted. The poor nations, then, have to utilize maximally their own resources. The projects should use the inputs that are available within the country. These are manpower and the natural resources. A careful manpower[19] resource mobilization planning is necessary along with natural resources like forestry[20] and other native vegetation, land cultivation, fisheries and other aquatic sea resources, rivers and sea waters. Geological conditions and availability of technical knowledge allow the development and extraction of minerals. This is what has been envisaged in Arusha Declaration. There are, of course, some problems and difficulties, which are inevitable under such circumstances of non-cooperation from the developed part of the world. These inputs will certainly lead the poor nations towards self-reliance, though it would take a longer period than it would have with cooperation. This will mean that economic development has to be started from the traditional way of life and eventually hammered out with the high dynamics of development. This has to be accomplished through successive stage development with a cross feedback linkage mechanism, starting from agriculture, agricultural mechanization, and rural industrialization.[21]

However, with the help of developed nation, the process can be accelerated. "Although both aid is needed and wanted, the country cannot allow itself to become dependent upon outside sources", said Derk Bryceson[22], Minister in the Government of Tanzania, The former Canadian Prime Minister, Lester Pearson[23] had to say, "From this crippling state of subjection, the only escape is the clean break the Japanese imposed on Western traders and missionaries in the 17th century—a strong version, if you like, of America's revolutionary break with the British trading system in 1776, a break comparative to Russia turning inwards in 1928 and launching the First Five-Year Plan." Today, the underdeveloped nations need a similar kind of transformation of the existing socio-cultural value systems in the aftermath of colonial oppression.

To sum up, with all these frustrations and bitterness and complications in the development process, let us be optimistic, and see if these strategies (Arusha Declaration[24]) and ideologies (Pearson[25] Report, Brandt Commission Report[26] and South Commission Report[27]) can be worked out together to eradicate hunger and poverty within the existing UN system.

At present, the main task of the UN has become like a 'Development Corporation', and this is especially true in the light of the Capacity Study, and the establishment of additional organs—UNCTAD and UNDP. In 1945, it had 51 members, of which three were African nations and four were Asian. In May 1983, it had 160 members, of which over 100 were developing countries. Its socio-economic development related aspects absorb about 80 per cent of its resources and about 90 per cent of its manpower. The effectiveness of the UN Development System is the only hope left, if any, as far as the role of external factors is concerned in the development process. In order to salvage anything from the recommendations of the Pearson and Brandt Reports, it is only the UN, which can form a 'coalition' with the ideologies expressed in the Arusha Declaration to accelerate the development process. The UN is a perfect organization to accomplish the goal. It has one link missing, and without this link the whole UN system is in a crippled state. The missing link is the lack of power and authority invested in the UN to implement its resolutions. Without this line, the system is unable to move. This missing link may encourage its member States, particularly those of the underdeveloped nations, to lose their faith in this system. It will then mean danger to its very existence. The ideas and ideals that were behind its formation after the World War II were that the world should not get involved in another horrible, terrible, and devastating war. If this missing link (that it cannot implement its resolutions by force, if necessary) is not provided, the UN cannot become an effective instrument in enforcing international peace and security. Ingvar Carlsson, Julius Nyerere, and Willy Brandt, in their joint communication in May 1991[28], said:

> "Whenever international law is broken, resolute action must be taken by the United Nations."

If the member States empower the UN unanimously to enforce its resolutions, the dream of a great humanitarian and a civil rights leader, Dr. Martin Luther King, Jr., will come true[29]:

> "...War will come to an end, that man will beat their swords into plough shares and their pruning hooks, that nations shall no longer rise up against nations, neither will they study war anymore."

Since 1989, there has been an unparalleled transformation of Eastern Europe and erstwhile USSR, which literally defies all imagination. Communism is wiped out from the face of

Eastern European countries and 15 independent sovereign republics have emerged out of what once was one of the two mighty super-powers known as the USSR till December 1991.

But the wiping out of communism from Europe and the emergence of 15 republics of the former USSR does not automatically spell the virtues of capitalism as it is practiced in Western Europe, USA, Canada, and other Western countries. Many countries in Asia, Africa and Latin America, the so called Third World, while they are not communist countries, are openly switching to free-market-based capitalist economic system of Western countries. This is just a folly of the highest order. The socio-economic conditions in the Third World countries are very different from those of the Eastern European countries and the former USSR.

A large majority of people in most of the Third world countries is unable to help themselves. Those who are not able to help themselves must be helped by the State. Equity and social justice criteria require it. In the cut-throat competition of free market economy, (in the West dubbed as "market-friendly strategy for development" by the World Bank in its 1991 Annual Report[30], entitled World Development Report 1991) the vast majority of impoverished masses in most of the Third World will have their socio-economic conditions from bad to one of wretchedness, a condition of life below human dignity. Where there is no equality in opportunity even at the basic primary education, basic health, and drinking water, not to mention gainful productive employment, the helpless people are bound to remain where they are, that is, perpetually poverty-stricken. To such unfortunate dejected people, only the State can help. They will not be able to survive in a "market-friendly strategy for development" which is being widely preached by the World Bank. The IMF and the World Bank combine has in the recent past emerged as a sort of remote control in the hands of Western powers. Through the mechanism of debt, aid, and arms, the combine conveniently controls the economies of the countries in the Third World. While the fact is that, as Kuldeep Nayyar[31] , a noted journalist and former High Commissioner of India in the UK wrote:

> "...But I do not know of any country that might have become prosperous with the help and formulae of the International Monetory Fund (IMF)."

There is the necessity for equity and social justice criteria in India, for nearly 10 per cent of the 840 million people in 1991 control nearly 70 per cent of the means of production and services.[32] Under the "market-friendly approach for development" of the Western countries, the socio-economic interests of these 10 per cent of the people will be well looked after, but the fate of the struggling 90 per cent of the population is doomed. Based on equity and social justice criteria, therefore, it is just a folly for governments in the Third World to switch over to capitalism of the type of the West. As far as India is concerned, Prabhat Joshi[33], a noted journalist and editor of *Jansatta*, a prestigious and widely circulated Hindi daily from New Delhi, rightly said that:

> "After the failure of communism in the former USSR and Eastern Europe, it is not a matter of shame but of a tragedy that we are now switching to Western capitalism from the Russian socialism. Just as the Russian socialist model was not capable to solve our problems in India, similarly the free market capitalist system of the West will also not be able to solve our problems.
>
> Who other than Mahatma Gandhi in this country understood that solution to a problem emerges only from the point from where the problem originates? Nothing can be achieved with borrowed keys. There is no way in India other than the Gandhian way."

In India, from the present mixed approach of the economy, based on both free market and State controlled, a switch to purely "market-friendly approach for development" is not bound to work, because in its present manifestation it will cater largely to the urban industrial complex only, leaving aside the fate of the majority of 80 per cent of the population in rural areas. What has not been tried since the dawn of independence, nearly five decades ago in 1947, is a self-reliant decentralized village economy, fulfilling the needs of the people who live in nearly 600,000 villages? After all, the soul of India lives in villages. Without the transformation of the rural areas, with its 80 per cent of largely illiterate and poverty-stricken masses, nothing is bound to succeed, as we have been witnessing for the last five decades since 1947, despite all of our efforts through Five-Year Plans.[34]

The "market-friendly strategy for development", as advocated by the World Bank, will only benefit the already well-off Western countries who, with 20 per cent of the total population of the world, consume over 80 per cent of the world's resources, and these 80 per cent of the world's total resources are in the Third World itself. The "market-friendly strategy for development" for the Third World is nothing but a mirage. The Western powers have coined this expression to control the economies of the countries in the Third World. This attempt will lead towards economic dependence on the money-lenders of the West through the mechanism of IMF and World Bank combine. Balraj Mehta, a noted Indian political thinker is of the view that[35]:

> "These economic reforms are being initiated in India at the instance of the Multinational Corporations (MNCs) in collusion with certain business houses, bureaucrats, and political leaders of India. This dangerous gang is pushing India towards dependency of neo-colonialism. Its results can never be good for Indian social, economic, and political institutions."

With the enhanced economic reforms in India since 1991 under the enforced globalization drive of the Western Powers, the poverty in India, South Asia and in developing countries is not at all decreased during these more than 10 years of so called reforms. Table 5.1 gives data on poverty in each country of South Asia. Table 5.2 gives similar data on various regions of the world. It is clear from these Tables that[36]:

> ...Poor people are active agents in their lives, but are often powerless to influence the social and economic factors that

Table 5.1: Population, GNP, Poverty, and HDI Rank in South Asian Countries

| *Country Region* | *Population 1999 millions* | *GNP Per Capita (US$ and Indian Rs.) 1999* | | *Human Devt. Index Rank Among 162 Countries in 2001* | *Population in Poverty 1995* | | *Population below Income Poverty Line %* | |
|---|---|---|---|---|---|---|---|---|
| | | *(In $)* | *(In Rs.)* | | *Number millions* | *$ 1 a Day (1993 PPP US$ 1983-99)* | *$ 1 a Day (1993 PPP US$ 1983-99)* | *National Poverty Line 1984-99* |
| India | 992.7 | 450 | 20,250 | 115 | 328 | 35 | 44.2 | 35.0 |
| Pakistan | 137.6 | 470 | 21,150 | 127 | 41 | 29 | 31.0 | 34.0 |
| Bangladesh | 134.6 | 370 | 16,650 | 132 | 55 | 46 | 29.1 | 35.6 |
| Nepal | 18.7 | 220 | 9,900 | 129 | 10 | 45 | 6.6 | 25.0 |
| Sri Lanka | 22.5 | 820 | 36,900 | 81 | 4 | 22 | 37.7 | 42.0 |
| Bhutan | 2.0 | 510 | 22,950 | 130 | NA | NA | - | - |
| Maldives | 0.3 | 1160 | 52,200 | 77 | NA | NA | - | - |
| South Asia | 1377.6 | 440 | 19,800 | - | 438 | 35 | - | - |

*Note:* Indian Rs. calculated at the exchange rate of Rs. 45 per US$.

*Sources:* Data extracted from:

(1) Mahbub ul Haq and Khadija Haq, *Human Development In South Asia 1998*, The Human Development Centre, Karachi, Pakistan, (Oxford University Press, Karachi, Pakistan, 1998).

(2) United Nations Development Programme, Human Development Report, 2000, (Oxford University Press, New York, 2000).

(3) United Nations Development Programme, Human Development Report, 2001, (Oxford University Press, New York, 2001).

(4) The World Bank, World Development Report, 2000/2001, (Oxford University Press, New York, 2000).

**Table 5.2:** Poverty in Various Regions of the World for 2000

| *Region* | *Poverty 1998 People Living on Less than $ 1 a Day/Rs. 45* | | *Poverty 1987 People Living on Less than $ 1 a Day/Rs. 45* | |
|---|---|---|---|---|
| | *Number millions* | *Per cent* | *Number millions* | *Per cent* |
| | WDR p 23 | | | |
| East Asia & Pacific | 278.3 | 15.3 | 417.5 | 26.6 |
| Excluding China | 65.1 | 11.3 | 114.1 | 23.9 |
| Europe and Central Asia | 24.0 | 5.1 | 1.1 | 0.2 |
| Latin America & Caribbean | 78.2 | 15.6 | 63.7 | 15.3 |
| Middle East & North Africa | 5.5 | 1.9 | 9.3 | 4.3 |
| *South Asia* | 522.0 | 40.0 | 474.4 | 44.9 |
| Sub-Saharan Africa | 290.9 | 46.3 | 217.2 | 46.6 |
| Total | 1,198.9 | 24.0 | 1,183.2 | 28.3 |
| Excluding China | 985.7 | 26.2 | 879.8 | 28.5 |

*Source:* The World Bank, World Development Report 2000/2001, Oxford University Press, New York, 2000, p. 23. The poverty line is $1.08 a day at 1993 PPP).

determine their well-being. ...The world has deep poverty amid plenty. Of the world's 6 billion people (in the year 2000) 2.8 billion—almost half-live on less than $2 a day, and 1.2 billion—a fifth-live on less than $1 a day, with 44 per cent living in South Asia.

In South Asia countries, percentage of population living below the poverty may have come down in the decade from nearly 45 per cent in 1987 to 40 per cent in 1998, but the fact remains that the absolute number of them has increased from 475 million to 522 million. So at the current rate of progress in implementing the poverty alleviation schemes, the poverty would never be out of the face of the South Asia.

### Human Development Index

The HDI measures the overall achievements in a country in three basic dimensions of human development longevity, knowledge and a decent standard of living. It is measured by life expectancy, educational attainment (adult literacy and combined primary, secondary and tertiary enrolment) and adjusted income per capita in purchasing power parity (PPP) US dollars. The HDI is a summary, not a comprehensive measure of human development. (*Human Development Report 2001*, UNDP, Oxford University Press, New York, 2001, p. 14).

### Human Poverty Index

While the HDI measures overall progress in a country in achieving human development, the human poverty index (HPI) reflects the distribution of progress and measures the backlog of deprivations that still exists. The HPI measures deprivation in the same dimensions of basic human development as the HDI (*Human Development Report 2001*, UNDP, Oxford University Press, New York, 2001, p. 14).

The public opinion of the impact of these reforms is reflected in the following to Surveys:

> So the impact of economic reforms is being literally nil on poverty reduction. As in-depth analysis of this impact of reforms on the economy is put forth by Mohan Guruswami[37]:

- Industrial growth in 1981-91 was 7.7 per cent. Since 1991-92 it has been 5.8 per cent.
- Agricultural growth, which averaged 4.04 per cent annually for the decade 1981-91, fell to 2.3 per cent annually for the period 1991-92.
- The annual electricity generation capacity growth fell to 3.5 per cent during 1991-99 as opposed to 12.4 per cent for 1981-91. Electricity generation growth fell from 17 per cent to 7.8 per cent for the corresponding period.
- Trade deficits have been growing exponentially. In 1980-81 the adverse balance was Rs. 5,838 crore In 1990-91 this was Rs. 10,645 crore. In 1998-99 it swelled to Rs. 55,478 crore.
- Poverty levels have remained constant at about 33 per

cent. Therefore the numbers living below the poverty line have swelled by 46.7 million to 326.04 million in 1999.

- Rupee: in 1981 the dollar was worth Rs. 8, in 1991 this changed to Rs. 18, and now to almost Rs. 44.

The World Bank and IMF have become the standard torchbearers of providing *prescriptions* for poverty alleviation in developing countries. An example of these prescriptions is given below:

***The new poverty reduction strategy initiative of the WB & IMF*[38]**

The poverty reduction strategy initiative of the World Bank and International Monetary Fund seeks to link external support to domestically developed, results-based poverty strategies. It is also intended to improve the effectiveness of World Bank and IMF relations (and those of other donors as well) with recipient countries. As important as the recipient country strategy is the process leading up to it. A broad, participatory dialogue with representatives of civil society and the private sector is expected to:

- Help national authorities develop a better understanding of the obstacles to poverty reduction and growth and devise good indicators of progress in poverty reduction.
- Deepen a shared vision of desired poverty reduction goals across society.
- Lead to formulation of priorities for public actions to achieve the desired poverty reduction outcomes.

Encourage the development of participatory processes for setting poverty reduction goals and monitoring implementation and progress.

While the actual form of the strategy will be decided by the country—there is no single blueprint—most strategies would likely include:

- Long-term goals for key poverty reduction targets, and the macroeconomic, structural, and institutional framework for achieving them.
- Mechanisms for monitoring and evaluating progress towards the poverty reduction targets, linked to public actions.
- A consistent policy and institutional framework that includes the underpinnings for rapid, sustained growth and poverty reduction (including macroeconomic policies, institutional reforms, sector strategies, and associated domestic and external financing needs).

***The World Bank considers, "four key areas of international action for poverty reduction***[39]

- Expanding market access in rich countries for developing countries' goods and services.
- Reducing the risk of economic crises.
- Encouraging the production of international public goods that benefit poor people.
- Ensuring a voice for poor countries and poor people in global forums."

***Global and regional patterns: income poverty and social indicators***[40]

Between 1987 and 1998 the share of the population in developing and transition economies living on less than $1 a day fell from 28 per cent to 24 per cent. This decline is below the rate needed to meet the international development goal of reducing extreme income poverty by half by 2015.

Because of population growth, the number of people in poverty hardly changed. But there are large regional variations in performance. East Asia and the Middle East and North Africa have reduced their numbers in poverty—East Asia dramatically so. But in all other regions the number of people living on less than $1 a day has risen. In South Asia, for example, the number of poor people rose over the decade, from 474 million to 522 million, even though the share of people in poverty fell from 45 per cent to 40 per cent. In Latin America and the Caribbean the number of poor people rose by about 20 per cent.

Two regions fared particularly badly. In Europe and Central Asia the number of poverty soared from 1.1 million to 24 million. In Sub-Saharan Africa the number of poor people increased from an already high 217 million to 291 million over the same period, leaving almost half the residents of that continent poor. ...These variations in regional performance are leading to a shift in the geographical distribution of poverty. In 1998 South Asia and Sub-Saharan Africa accounted for around 70 per cent of the population living on less than $1 a day, up 10 percentage points from 1987.

### *The World Bank strategy for poverty reduction*[41]

The approach to reducing poverty has evolved over the past 50 years in response to deepening understanding of the complexity of development. In the 1950s and 1960s many viewed large investments in physical, capital and infrastructure as the primary means of development.

In the 1970s awareness grew that physical capital was not enough, and that at least as important were health and education. World Development Report 1980 articulated this understanding and argued that improvements in health and education were important not only in their own right but also to promote growth in the incomes of poor people.

The 1980s saw another shift of emphasis following the debt crisis and global recession and the contrasting experience of East Asia and Latin America, South Asia, and Sub-Saharan Africa. Emphasis was placed on improving economic management and allowing greater play for market forces. World Development Report 1990: Poverty proposed a two-part strategy: promoting labour-intensive growth through economic openness and investment in infrastructure and providing basic services to poor people in health and education.

In the 1990s governance and institutions moved towards centre stage—as did issues of vulnerability at the local and national levels. This report builds on the earlier strategies in the light of the cumulative evidence and experience of the past decade—and in the light of the changed global context. It proposes a strategy for attacking poverty in three ways: promoting opportunity, facilitating empowerment, and enhancing security.

*Promoting opportunity:* Poor people consistently emphasize the centrality of material opportunities. This means jobs, credit, roads, electricity, markets for their produce, and the schools, water, sanitation, and health services that underpin the health and skills essential for work. Overall economic growth is crucial for generating opportunity.

*Facilitating empowerment:* The choice and implementation of public actions that are responsive to the needs of poor people depend on the interaction of political, social, and other institutional processes. Access to market opportunities and to public sector services is often strongly influenced by state and social institutions, which must be responsive and accountable to poor people.

*Enhancing security:* Reducing vulnerability—to economic shocks, natural disasters, ill health, disability, and personal violence—is an intrinsic part of enhancing well-being and encourages investment in human capital and in higher-risk, higher-return activities. This requires effective national action to manage the risk of economy wide shocks and effective mechanisms to reduce the risks faced by poor people, including health-and weather-related risks.

About these prescriptions on poverty alleviating strategies of the World Bank and the IMF, a noted Newspaper of India, *Times of India* wrote in its editorial[42]:

> But it seems that an organization which has supported statism in the developing world since its inception—the World Bank is an architect of failed policy—is loath to admit it.

Professor T.N. Srinivasan[43]: Who teaches economics at the University of Maryland in the USA, while commenting on World Bank's " Strategy for poverty reduction," simply felt that "*...The bank has wandered into areas for which it has neither a mandate nor competence.*"

All in all, the impact of globalization on the economies of developing countries is nothing but to destroy their infrastructure, i.e. with these *prescriptions* of IMF and the World Bank, the plight of the poor countries gets from bad to worse.

Joseph Stiglitz an eminent economist and Noble Laureate, who had worked for the World Bank, called these reforms as a four point formula to destroy a nation, as reported by Sucheta Dalal[44] in her thought provoking article:

> On October 10, *The Observer* of London carried an interview with *Joseph Stiglitz, the Nobel Prize winning* former Economist of the World Bank who had been shown the door by that hallowed organization. Stiglitz, in his usual scathing manner talked about how *the IMF-World Bank and the World Trade Organization are interchangeable masks of a single governance system serving the rich nations' agenda.* He talked of how the Bank prescribes the exact same four-point programme for all nations and ends up destroying their economies.
>
> *Privatization:* Stiglitz calls is *'Barbarization'*. He says politicians and officials have happily flogged off their electricity and water companies, lured by the 10 per cent commission paid for 'shaving a few billion off the sale price of national assets'.
>
> *Capital Market Liberalization:* Stiglitz calls this the *'Hot Money'* cycle. Along with the flow of investment capital, it channels cash for speculation in markets currency and real estate, which can disappear equally fast. When that happens, the IMF asks these nations to hike interest rates, in order to 'seduce speculations into returning a nation's own capital funds'. He cites the hot money tidal waves in Asia and Latin America as examples.
>
> *Market-Based Pricing:* Stiglitz calls it a fancy term for raising prices on food, water and cooking gas leading to what he calls *'The IMF riot'*. Indonesia, Ecuador and Bolivia exploded into riots over fuel, food and water prices.

*Free Trade:* Stiglitz likens free trade WTO style to the *Opium Wars* as it allows MNC to fleece people in poor countries by charging usurious prices for branded medicine and other services.

*India is more than half way through the implementation of this four-point recipe,* but there are interesting differences as well.

*Barbarization,* appears in a more vicious and reverse *avatar* in India. Politicians have persistently blocked efforts to privatize public sector companies in oil, steel, and power, aviation and OCBs. Indian *black money* flowed out of the country and was re-routed into the market for speculation through FSSs and OCBs. ...If *market-based pricing* has not exactly kicked off, it is because greed and infighting between private sector operators had not allowed the privatization of utilities to take off. ...The *opening of our markets* has meant inefficient and protected family run Indian companies and the small-scale sector have been badly hit by the free flow of cheap imports.

## NOTES

1. Prabhas Joshi, *Jansatta* (Hindi daily), New Delhi, 5-10-1991, p. 6. This passage of Joshi has been translated by the author from the original in Hindi. Joshi is editor of *Jansatta,* a widely circulated newspaper from New Delhi.
2. Frans J. Schuurman, Globalization and Development Studies: Introducing the Challenges, in Frans J. Schuurman, Ed., *Globalization and Development Studies: Challenges for the 21st Century,* Vistaar Publications (A division of Sage Pub.), New Delhi, 2001, p. 8.
3. Kristoffel Lieten, Multinationals and Development: Revisiting the Debate, in Frans J. Schuurman, Ed., *Globalization and Development Studies: Challenges for the 21st Century,* Vistaar Publications (A division of Sage Pub.), New Delhi, 2001, p. 112.
4. Jozsef Bognar, "An unbalanaced economy may bring a Crises," in *CERES Magazine,* FAO of the United Nations, Rome, Italy, Sept.-Oct. 1969, p. 52.
5. The proceedings were published in Frans J. Schuurman, Ed., *Globalization and Development Studies: Challenges for the 21st Century,* Vistaar Publications (A division of Sage Pub.), New Delhi, 2001.

6. Reinhart Kossler, Globalization and Human Rights: Some Developmental Reflections, in *Ibid.*, p. 83.
7. Frans J. Schuurman, Globalization and Development Studies: Introducing the Challenges, in *Ibid.*, p. 8.
8. Kristoffel Lieten, Multinationals and Development: Revisiting the Debate, in *Ibid.*, p. 104.
9. Reinhart Kossler, Globalization and Human Rights: Some Developmental Reflections, in *Ibid.*, p. 90.
10. Ton van Naerssen, Cities and the Globalization of Urban Development Policy, in *Ibid.*, p. 183.
11. Frans J. Schuurman, *The Nation-State, Emancipatory Spaces and Development Studies in the Global Era*, p. 63.
12. Kristoffel Lieten, Multinationals and Development: Revisiting the Debate, p. 112.
13. Raul Streeten, "Improving the Climate", in *CERES Magazine*, FAO of the United Nations, Rome, Italy, March-April, 1969; p. 58.
14. Quoted by S.G. Sardesai, "Achievements and Difficulties of Non-Alignment", in *World Marxist Review*, Toronto, March 1974; p. 80.
15. *Partners in Development*, (New York: Praeger Pub., 1969).
16. Hons Singer, "The Outlook for the Poor World", in New Internationalist Devon Press, Berkshire, England, July 1973, p. 18.
17. The Arusha Declaration marked a turning point in Tanzanian politics. For the text of this Declaration, see Julius K. Nyerere, *Freedom and Socialism*, (Dar-es Salaam: Oxford University Press, 1968), pp. 231-50.
18. *Ibid*, p. 235.
19. Sures Chandra Jain, *The Indigenous Resources for Rural Development: agricultural mechanization and rural industrialization*, Concept Publishing Co., New Delhi, 2004.
20. *Ibid.*, Chapter 5, "Utilization of Natural Resources".
21. *Ibid.*, Chapter 2, "Agricultural Mechanization and Rural Industrialization".
22. Derek Bryceson, "Tanzania Says yes but ...", in *CERES Magazine*, FAO of the United Nations, Rome, Italy, May-June, 1968; p. 32.
23. L.B. Pearson, "Pearson on Pearson Report", in *CERES Magazine*, *op. cit.*, p. 24.
24. *See* above footnote 17 (17n).
25. *Partners in Development*, (New York: Praeger Pub., 1969).
26. *North-South: A Programme for Survival*, (Cambridge Mass: The M.I.T. Press, 1980).
27. The Challenge to the South: The Report of the South Commission, (New York: Oxford University Press, 1990), pp. 226-28.
28. *The Hindustan Times*, New Delhi, 16-5-1991, p. 13.
29. Part of Quote in Janothan Power, Development Economics, (London, Longman, 1971), p. 3.

30. World Development Report, 1991, The World Bank, Washington DC, 1991, p. 6.
31. *Rajasthan Patrika* (Hindi daily), Jaipur, 17-7-1991, p. 6. (Original in Hindi)
32. Data are taken from an Editorial in *Dainik Bhaskar* (Hindi daily), Bhopal, 27-12-1991, p. 4.
33. *Jansatta* (Hindi daily), New Delhi, 5-10-1991; p. 6. ...Translated by the author from the original in Hindi.
34. On these issues, *see* the author's book; *The Indigenous Resources For Rural Development: agricultural mechanization and rural industrialization.*
35. *Rajasthan Patrika* (Hindi daily), Jaipur, 26-7-1991, p. 6. (Translated by the author from the original in Hindi).
36. The World Bank, World Development Report 2000/2001, Oxford University Press, New York, 2000, p 3. The poverty line is $1.08 a day at 1993 PPP.
37. Mohan Guruswamy, The sad face of liberalisation: After almost 10 years, all key indicators tell us that the New Economic Policy of 1991 has decelerated India's growth, *Indian Express*, April 11, 2000, p. 11 (Mr. Guruswamy is a former adviser to the FM).
38. The World Bank, World Development Report 2000/2001, Oxford University, Press, New York, 2000, p. 195.
39. *Ibid.*, p. 179.
40. *Ibid.*, pp. 21-23.
41. *Ibid.*, pp. 6-7.
42. Editorial, Go Home World Bank, *The Economic Times*, New Delhi, September 29, 2000, p. 12.
43. T.N. Srinivasan, WDR 2000-01: A poor report on poverty, *The Economic Times*, New Delhi, September 28, 2000, p. 7.
44. Sucheta Dalal, The four-point formula do destroy a nation, *Indian Express*, New Delhi, 15-10-2001 (Dak), p. 10.

# Index